Empath

How Empaths and Highly Sensitive People Can Thrive by Harnessing Their Gifts and Psychic Abilities

© Copyright 2022 - All rights reserved.

The content contained within this book may not be reproduced, duplicated, or transmitted without direct written permission from the author or the publisher.

Under no circumstances will any blame or legal responsibility be held against the publisher, or author, for any damages, reparation, or monetary loss due to the information contained within this book, either directly or indirectly.

Legal Notice:

This book is copyright protected. It's only for personal use. You cannot amend, distribute, sell, use, quote, or paraphrase any part, or the content within this book, without the consent of the author or publisher.

Disclaimer Notice:

Please note the information contained within this document is for educational and entertainment purposes only. All effort has been executed to present accurate, up-to-date, reliable, complete information. No warranties of any kind are declared or implied. Readers acknowledge that the author is not engaging in the rendering of legal, financial, medical, or professional advice. The content within this book has been derived from various sources. Please consult a licensed professional before attempting any techniques outlined in this book.

By reading this document, the reader agrees that under no circumstances is the author responsible for any losses, direct or indirect, that are incurred as a result of the use of the information contained within this document, including, but not limited to, errors, omissions, or inaccuracies.

Free limited time bonus

Stop for a moment. I have a free bonus set up for you. The problem is that we forget 90% of everything that we read after 7 days. Crazy fact, right? Here's the solution: we've created a printable, 1-page pdf summary for this book that you're reading now. All you have to do to get your free pdf summary is to go to the following website: **https://livetolearn.lpages.co/silviahill/**
Once you do, it will be intuitive. Enjoy, and thank you!

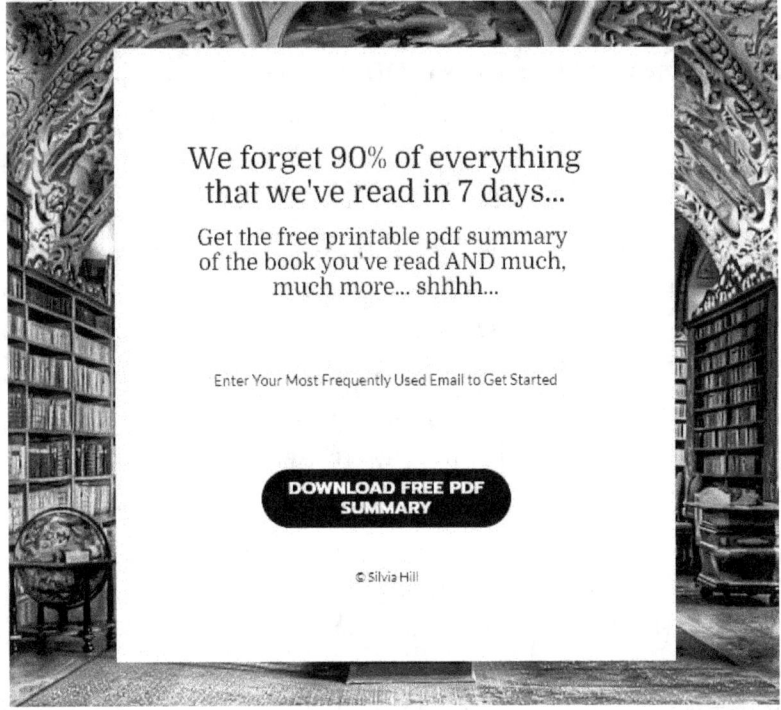

Contents

INTRODUCTION 1
CHAPTER 1: EMPATHY: AN INTRODUCTION 3
    WHAT IS EMPATHY? 6
    DIFFERENT TYPES OF EMPATHY 7
    WHAT DOES AN EMPATH FEEL? 9
CHAPTER 2: THE ABILITIES OF AN EMPATH 14
    THE ABILITIES OF AN EMPATH 16
    WHY BEING AN EMPATH IS A GIFT 20
    TYPES OF EMPATHS 22
    INTROVERTED VS. EXTROVERTED EMPATHS 24
    COMMON CAREERS ADOPTED BY EMPATHS 25
CHAPTER 3: ARE YOU AN EMPATH? 27
    LIFE AS AN EMPATH 30
    QUIZ: AM I AN EMPATH? 33
    WHAT TYPE OF EMPATH AM I? 34
CHAPTER 4: EMPATHS VS. HIGHLY SENSITIVE PEOPLE 37
    WHAT IS A HIGHLY SENSITIVE PERSON (HSP)? 38
    HOW TO KNOW IF YOU'RE AN HSP 39
    YOUR SCORE 41
    EMPATHS VS. HSPS 41
    WHAT ABOUT INTROVERSION AND SHYNESS? 43

- When Empathy, High Sensitivity, and Introversion Overlap 44
- The Opposites of an Empath, HSP, and Introvert Are...? 45
- Are You an Empath or an HSP? 46
- Common Challenges Empaths and HSPs Face 48

CHAPTER 5: THE EMPATH AND THE SELF: ADDICTIONS 50
- What Is Addiction? 51
- Types of Addiction 51
- Why Are Empaths More Susceptible to Addiction? 55
- Symptoms of Addiction 57
- Self-Assessment 58
- How to Cope with Addiction 59

CHAPTER 6: THE WORKING EMPATH 63
- How Empaths Interact in the Workplace 64
- How to Cope with Demanding Bosses and Tough Work Situations 68
- What to Consider before Taking a Job 71

CHAPTER 7: EMPATHS IN LOVE 73
- Why Do You Struggle in Relationships? 74
- How to Deal with Problems in Relationships 78
- How to Stop Absorbing Emotions 81

CHAPTER 8: PARENTING AND RAISING EMPATH CHILDREN 83
- Signs of an Empathic Child 85
- How to Give Their Empathic Nature Direction 87
- Tips for Parenting 89

CHAPTER 9: EMPATHS VS. NARCISSISTS 93
- Who Are Narcissists? 93
- Traits of a Narcissist 95
- Types of Narcissism 97
- The Fatal Attraction of an Empath and a Narcissist 98
- How to Tell if Your Partner Is a Narcissist 99
- How to Deal with a Narcissist 102

CHAPTER 10: UNDERSTANDING YOUR FEELINGS 104
- Signs That an Empath Is Overwhelmed 105
- Healthy Coping Mechanisms 108

CHAPTER 11: SETTING BOUNDARIES 115
- INTERACTIONS AS AN EMPATH 116
- TYPES OF BOUNDARIES 117
- WHAT BOUNDARIES ARE 119
- WHAT BOUNDARIES ARE NOT 120
- HOW TO SET BOUNDARIES 120

CHAPTER 12: HOW TO CONTROL YOUR EMOTIONS 125
- ABSORBING EMOTIONS 126
- UNDERSTAND THE EMOTION 126

CHAPTER 13: EMPATH WELLNESS 135
- EMPATHY AND PHYSICAL WELL-BEING 136
- PHYSICAL EFFECTS 136
- EMOTIONAL EFFECTS 137
- THE BODY'S RESPONSE TO ANXIETY AND DEPRESSION 138
- DIET AND EMPATHY 139
- WHY EMPATHS FEEL DRAINED 141

CHAPTER 14: MASTERING YOUR MENTAL ENERGY 148
- SITUATIONS THAT AFFECT MENTAL ENERGY 149
- UTILIZING YOUR MENTAL ENERGY 150
- RECOGNIZING EMPATHY SKILLS 156

CHAPTER 15: EMPATH IN A CRUEL WORLD 160
- ADDRESSING SOCIETAL FEARS 162
- FEELING MISUNDERSTOOD 163
- FEELING UNWANTED 164
- FEELING VALUELESS 165
- FEELING UNLOVED 166
- NOT FEELING ACCEPTED 166
- THE INABILITY TO JUST "GET OVER IT" 167
- NEWS AND SOCIETY 167
- SELF-PROTECTION METHODS 167

CHAPTER 16: EMBRACING YOUR SPIRIT 170
- WHAT IS SPIRITUALITY AND WHY IS IT IMPORTANT? 171
- THE BENEFITS OF CONNECTING WITH YOUR SPIRIT 173
- MEDITATION METHODS 174

CONCLUSION	183
HERE'S ANOTHER BOOK BY SILVIA HILL THAT YOU MIGHT LIKE	185
FREE LIMITED TIME BONUS	186
REFERENCES	187

Introduction

Empathy is a feature of the human personality that manifests itself in varying degrees and can impact a person's life in more than one way. Simply feeling someone else's position and being able to place yourself in their shoes is empathy, but the accuracy with which you can do this and the impact of this empathy on your own life is something that needs your attention. This book will explore all the ideas, concepts, pros, and cons of being an empath and even living with one. We all have some degree of empathy. On one end of the spectrum is a person who feels empathy so strongly that it can often override their own emotions, becoming a hindrance in their lives. At the other extreme are people classified as psychopaths who live in their own shell, and even if they want to, they are unable to feel anything for another person. The average person lies somewhere in the middle of this spectrum. We will look at why and how empathy is developed in a person and how it can influence their life.

Similarly, understanding the level of empathy in people around you is also a vital tool. We all have different emotional needs, and those with a higher level of empathy are different from those with a lower level of empathy. To communicate and co-exist with these people appropriately, we need to know how we can connect with them at a deeper emotional level. When you have a spouse, a child, a parent, or a coworker who has a different place on the empathy spectrum than you, it can be challenging to get along with them and develop a meaningful relationship.

In this book, we will look at various tools, techniques, and strategies that you can use to more effectively communicate and connect with individuals who are different kinds of empaths. We will look at the key things that make an empath different from other emotional conditions, such as a highly sensitive person. Based on the latest research, we will also look at how an empath can even be physically different. They are literally wired differently, and we will look at how this influences their lives and the people around them.

If you fall into the empathy category, this will impact your entire life, it's part of your personality, your mind, and it's something that cannot be looked at in isolation. This book will look at all the different aspects of life from the lens of an empath and how you can make the most of each situation that you come across. Whether facing challenges at work or dealing with intimate relationships, this book is a complete roadmap of how you can navigate life as an empath.

If you are looking for an easy-to-follow guide, one that's filled with helpful advice from people who have actually been there and done that, this is the resource you need. If you are ready to improve your life today, let's get started with the empath's journey.

Chapter 1: Empathy: An Introduction

"I know how you feel." This is a sentence that so many people say when we're sad or crying. We just assume that they are trying to be nice because how can anyone really know or understand what we are going through? Well, an empath can.

An empath is very sensitive and is unusually attuned to other people's emotions and feelings. In other words, they don't only sympathize, but they can feel what everyone around them is feeling as well. They are the last people you ask to put themselves in your shoes because they are already there. For instance, when at a funeral, an empath can take on other people's feelings and sense their loss, pain, and sadness. If they are at a wedding, they can feel everyone else's happiness and excitement as well. Depending on the situation, it can feel like either a gift or a curse. It's a gift when it helps the empath establish healthy professional and personal relationships. They can emphasize more than most people and tell what someone is feeling by looking at their face. When someone is upset or going through something, but they smile and pretend to be ok, they can fool anyone in the room except an empath, who can see through anyone's mask.

Empaths can feel other people's feelings because their brains function differently from most people. An empath's brain contains highly-responsive mirror neurons that trigger feelings like compassion and allow empaths to mirror the emotions of the people around them. An empath can be very sensitive to the electromagnetic waves emitted by other people's hearts or brains, allowing the empath to feel their emotions on a deeper level. Simply put, an empath is like a walking sponge that absorbs other people's emotions, whether negative or positive, which can be overwhelming at times. For this reason, empaths need to set healthy boundaries to protect themselves from the overwhelming emotions they feel when they are around others. In the coming chapters, we will discuss in detail how to set healthy boundaries.

Being an empath has many advantages. If you are an empath, you'll find making new friends and maintaining those friendships quite easy. This is because empaths are great listeners, are always there for their friends whenever needed, are generous, and have big hearts, all of which are qualities that make a person a great friend. But being an empath can be a curse as well. All of these qualities that make them such great friends can take a toll on their mental health. Since empaths can feel what everyone is feeling, they will be attuned to their friends' emotions. So, when your friend comes to you with a problem, and they are feeling anxious, sad, or angry, you will find yourself taking on these emotions as well and thus feeling extremely overwhelmed. The problem that empaths face is that they tend to adopt other people's issues as if they are their own. So, when someone comes to them with a problem or asks them a huge favor, they just can't say no even if it's inconvenient. Empaths find it hard to set proper boundaries, which is why they cannot say no, no matter how big the ask is.

Spending time with other people can drain an empath. Think of an empath like a battery that's constantly working when surrounded by people - eventually - it will drain and require recharging. For this reason, you'll find that most empaths are actually introverts. Introverts, by nature, like to spend some time alone to recharge after spending time around other people. If introverts don't recharge, they can feel anxious or even depressed. Additionally, empaths can also suffer from social anxiety because of how overwhelmed they get in a crowd. Other people's chatter and noises can affect the empath's sensitive nature. An empath will feel more relaxed and in their element when they are in a quiet place like nature.

In addition to panic attacks, an empath can also feel tired, depressed, and anxious when they are overwhelmed by other people's emotions or in a stressful situation. They may also exhibit physical symptoms like headaches, exhaustion, and fast heart rate. When an empath takes on other people's emotions, they usually have trouble differentiating these feelings from their own, which is why they exhibit these mental and physical symptoms. To avoid feeling overwhelmed, an empath needs to be able to recognize their own feelings and separate them from other people's feelings.

What Is Empathy?

To better understand what it feels like to be an empath, you'll first need to have a better understanding of what empathy is. Empathy is the ability to put yourself in someone else's place so you can understand their thoughts and feelings and see things from their perspective. Not to be confused with sympathy, which is being moved or touched by someone else's feelings while keeping an emotional distance. For instance, if an empath sees a person mourning the loss of a pet, they may be able to understand their pain by easily putting themselves in this person's shoes and feel their loss, even though they have never lost a pet themselves – or even have one. However, a regular person may simply sympathize by feeling sorry but without a deep understanding or feeling the person's emotions. Feeling empathy doesn't require you to go through the same experiences or live in the same circumstances to understand other people's feelings. Your brain will simply mirror their emotions, and you will feel them as if they are your own.

It's easy for most people to understand their own emotions and see things from their own perspectives. However, stepping into someone else's shoes may not be as easy. You need empathy to understand and feel exactly other people's emotions. That said, just as there are people in the world who aren't honest or caring, you will also encounter people who aren't empathetic. You will find people who are dismissive towards other people's feelings or get aggressive or angry when they see someone suffering or crying. For instance, we hear in the news people committing the most horrendous acts, and we wonder how they can do this without feeling any remorse? Notorious serial killer Ted Bundy didn't have interpersonal empathy and didn't feel any pity for his victims or guilt for any of the crimes he committed. Empathy isn't universal, so don't expect people to feel the same way you do or respond to other people's pain and suffering like you do.

That said, it isn't just serial killers or criminals who cannot feel empathy. If you take a look around you, you'll probably notice a few people who are unable to feel or even sympathize with other people's pain and suffering. Some managers refuse to give an employee a day off to attend a family member's funeral, husbands who can't seem to relate or understand their wives' struggles with raising a new baby alone at home.

As we have mentioned, not everyone can feel empathy. One of the main things that influence a person's ability to feel empathy is genetics. As a matter of fact, women are more likely to feel empathy and understand other people's emotions than men. So, does that mean that empaths are born, not created? Well, there is no denying that genetics play a huge role, but your environment and social interactions can help you develop empathy, among other things.

For instance, a child raised by one or two empath parents will more than likely develop empathy as well. This is because they grew up watching and observing their parents' emphasis on their needs. They were taught the importance of emotions and how to build relationships and connections with others. When a parent creates a connection with their child and establishes a shared experience, this will enable the child to connect with other people's emotions and develop empathy.

Different Types of Empathy

Renowned psychologists Paul Ekman and Daniel Goleman have broken down empathy into three categories.

- **Emotional Empathy**

    Emotional empathy allows you to feel other people's emotions as if they are your own and put yourself in their position. You may even feel their physical pain as well. For instance, if you are sitting with a friend and they get a paper cut, you may cringe or even yell "Ouch" as if you are the one who cut their finger. You are basically feeling whatever the people around you are feeling, whether physical or emotional, on some level. These emotions cause you to feel worried or distressed when someone you care about is going through something.

You will find that great friends, supportive parents, compassionate leaders, and caregivers have all developed emotional empathy. But this type of empathy can overwhelm you and impact your emotional well-being because you'll be so concerned with other people's problems you'll start ignoring your own.

- **Cognitive Empathy**

Cognitive empathy gives you the ability to understand people's mental states. Simply put, you can understand what they are thinking in any given situation. Cognitive empathy is different from emotional empathy because you will find that you can put yourself in another person's shoes without taking on or feeling their emotions. Therefore, you will respond to other people's emotions using logic rather than feelings. In other words, you won't be clouded by your emotions, which can make a person seem cold in some situations.

Cognitive empathy can help you in your personal and professional life. Since it gives you the chance to understand what another person is thinking and get inside their head, negotiate business deals, resolve conflicts, and motivate your team.

- **Compassionate Empathy**

Compassionate empathy is the balance between emotional and cognitive empathy. It connects your heart with your brain to create a middle ground to understand both a person's emotions and thoughts in any given situation. In addition to feeling and understanding what a person is going through, compassionate empathy will also move you to act to solve other people's problems. This type is considered the best and most helpful of the three types we have mentioned because it allows you to consider the intellectual and emotional side of a person so you can respond properly.

What Does an Empath Feel?

Empathy is about feeling other people's feelings but is that it? An empath has various emotions and thoughts when they are around other people. They may not be able to recognize these feelings since they are usually overwhelmed and can't distinguish their feelings from those of others. Understanding an empath's feelings will give you a deeper understanding of your abilities.

- **Art Can Affect You**

  Do you cry when you listen to a sad song? Do you get emotional when love conquers all at the end of a movie? Are you able to feel the emotions behind a painting or a picture? If you answer yes to any of these, then this means that you are easily affected by different types of arts like paintings, movies, or songs because, most certainly, you are an empath.

In addition to art, tragic news and violent scenes can also negatively impact an empath. If you are watching news happening on the other side of the world or a violent scene in a movie, you will feel the pain as if it's happening to you. This can be extremely overwhelming and affect your mental health. For this reason, try to avoid the news and violent media content as much as you can.

- **You Identify as an Introvert**

Unlike extroverts who feel more energetic when surrounded by crowds, an empath will probably identify more with introversion. They feel overwhelmed in crowds, so they choose to be around one or two people to avoid feelings of being overwhelmed. As mentioned, after spending time with people, an empath prefers to spend time alone to recharge. You can recharge by taking a walk in nature, sitting by yourself in a quiet room, or practicing your favorite hobby. One of the most famous introverts in history is the late famous painter Vincent Van Gogh who found refuge and escape from the loud world in his paintings.

- **Intimate Relationships Can Be Difficult**

There is no denying that every relationship has its struggles. However, for someone who can feel every little thing their partner is feeling and can tell when they are lying, being intimate in a close relationship can be overwhelming; having someone sharing your space can be challenging for an empath like you. Your home is where you spend some time alone to recharge, so having someone with you at all times and their emotions just waiting for you to absorb can be challenging. For this reason, you may find that many empaths prefer to be single. On the other hand, others manage to have successful relationships by learning to set boundaries and finding a person that respects these boundaries.

- **You Feel People's Physical Pain**

As mentioned earlier, being an empath doesn't mean only feeling other people's emotions, but you can also feel their physical pain as well. If you are in a hospital or around a friend who is injured or sick, you may feel their pain as if it's your own. We don't mean here that you will feel worried about them or sympathize with their pain; we mean that you will feel the exact pain they are feeling. For instance, if a friend of yours was in a car accident and they broke their left arm, you may feel pain in your left arm as well. The neurons in your brain will mirror what the other person is experiencing physically in your body. It's as if you are the one who was in the accident and broke your arm.

- **Experiencing Sudden Emotions**

You are out with a friend having lunch at a restaurant, you are joking and laughing, and suddenly, you feel sad. You don't understand why or how you are feeling this emotion. When an empath is around people, they can take on anyone's emotion at any time. It can be the waiter serving your food who got upset about something at work or a person at the next table who just received terrible news. As an empath, when you are in a public place, you can take on anyone's feelings without even trying to.

- **You Seek Peace and Quiet**

The vibe or a feeling of a room can have a massive effect on an empath. They prefer peaceful and quiet environments where they can recharge and calm themselves. This is why you will find yourself gravitating towards beautiful and quiet places like outside in nature, a garden, a museum, or a beautifully decorated room. You will be able to flourish in these places. On the other hand, loud and chaotic environments can drain your energy.

- **You Always Care**

Empaths always care about other people. When they pick up on what others are feeling, they have the urge to want to help them, and they act accordingly. If you can't find a way to help someone in distress, you will feel very disappointed. It's always great to lend a hand and help others, but you should also pay attention to your needs and energy, or you will burn out and won't be able to help others or yourself.

- **You Avoid Conflict**

Empaths hate conflicts and will do anything to avoid them. Since they are infinitely more sensitive, they may not be able to handle conflicts. They can't help feeling hurt and take comments personally. When an empath is arguing with someone, they aren't only dealing with their emotions but also with the other person's emotions and absorbing them. This can be very overwhelming.

- **You Feel Different**

Although you can feel what others are feeling, you will struggle with relating to other people. Absorbing people's emotions and feeling them as your own may make you feel you don't fit in because you constantly struggle to understand all these emotions you are absorbing. You could start to feel alone and that no one understands you, and possibly, you will keep your emotions and sensitivities to yourself to avoid feeling judged for being different. However, empathy is a unique gift that you should never hide or be ashamed of.

- **You Can't Set Boundaries**

Learning to set boundaries is essential for any empath. However, many empaths struggle with doing it because empaths can't simply press a button that will stop them from absorbing others' emotions or wanting to help them. The sensitive empath may think that they don't care about helping other people if they set boundaries. On the contrary, setting boundaries allows you to protect your mental health and energy from feeling overwhelmed by your and others' emotions. When you take care of yourself, you will be able to take care of the people in your life.

Being an empath is a beautiful gift that many people have used to help themselves and others create something beautiful. You will find many sensitive artists to be empaths - Ed Sheeran uses his gift to create beautiful, authentic, and relatable lyrics. You will feel that he is describing your emotions. Nelson Mandela was another excellent example of an empath who felt others' pain, so he sacrificed his own needs to help them. Mother Teresa and Mahatma Gandhi are also empaths who lived their lives in the service of others. The world can use more empathy, and it's a good thing that there are more empaths like you around.

We need more empaths in our lives. People who care, love, and heal. This is a unique gift that will allow you to make a difference in the world. We know that being an empath can be a struggle sometimes, but hopefully, in the coming chapters, we will be able to help you to understand your gift better and to learn to use your abilities while setting healthy boundaries.

Chapter 2: The Abilities of an Empath

Most empaths believe that having heightened sensitivity and awareness is burdensome. The thing is that they don't take the time to learn more about their abilities and understand how gifted they are, which is why they try to shut their empathy off. You must learn how valuable your abilities as an empath are. Learning more about your unique traits and how they set you apart from the rest of the world will help you appreciate your gift and come to see that your high sensitivity puts you at an advantage. There will be times when you feel no one understands you or reciprocates your ability to cater to others' physical and emotional needs. However, embarking on the journey to self-discovery and learning about the fantastic upsides of being highly empathetic can help you shift your view.

Being highly sensitive in the world we live in is tough. You may have been called an introvert or a buzz kill when you just needed some alone time. You may have had people take advantage of your compassion or inability to just say "no," or constantly struggle to identify which feelings are yours. Being an empath comes with endless emotional fatigue and intense waves of emotions. Your tendency to care about the most minor details, which also causes you to feel upset over those small details, may have thrown others off. It's hard to communicate with others when their feelings deeply influence yours or when they don't understand why you can't just "let things go." It comes as no surprise that you've always thought that something was wrong with you.

It's about time that you let go of the false belief about yourself and realize that you're not an alien. You can do that by delving deep into your authentic nature as an empath. It also helps to see that you aren't alone and work toward accepting your heightened awareness and sensitivities. Fortunately, this book will teach you many helpful methods that will allow you to use your abilities in ways to benefit you rather than drain you.

In this chapter, you will discover that everything you believed was wrong with you is actually your key to making the world a better place. You'll learn all about your abilities as an empath and why you are gifted. This chapter also covers the different types of empaths and the differences between introverted and extroverted. Finally, you'll come across a list of common careers adopted by empaths.

The Abilities of an Empath

So many online resources focus on the downsides of being an empath and the things that highly aware and sensitive people should take care of. This is perhaps why you, and numerous other individuals who possess this incredible ability, underestimate the powers you have. It's why countless empaths try to get rid of their abilities to "fit in" and just experience life like the rest of humanity. The fact is that there are numerous reasons why it's incredible to be an empath. Perhaps another reason you forget to give yourself enough credit's that you're more concerned about the well-being of everyone else. Once you verse yourself in your abilities, you will become a compelling force in your community. The most significant proof is that some of the most influential historical figures, such as Mother Theresa, Nelson Mandela, and Mahatma Gandhi, were empaths. The following are some of the abilities that empaths possess.

- **Highly Analytical**

Empaths are excellent at viewing and analyzing situations deeply, from all sides. A non-empath is likely to see a situation from only their own perspective or at least have certain biases. However, empaths can look into situations from the points of view of everyone involved. Empaths are likely to pick up on symbols and themes, making them the center of pivotal interactions. Their insights and ability to see right through things and straight to the point allow them to disengage from events to analyze the root of the issue. This means that they're likely to develop ideal solutions and compromises for any type of problem or disagreement. They are very helpful at fixing the problems or offering advice to the people they care about. This ability makes empaths prominent visionary leaders.

- **Very Intuitive**

Empaths are very compassionate and may find it hard to say no to any requests for their help, even when it costs them mentally or emotionally. Fortunately, empaths are blessed with highly intuitive abilities that can help them protect themselves from energy vampires and self-absorbed individuals. Empaths are very in tune with their own feelings and emotions and those of others, which helps them keep negative situations at arm's length. You probably often have this inexplicable and robust gut feeling if you're an empath. This is your intuition trying to communicate with you, so be sure to listen.

- **Empathy Over Long-Distance**

We've all experienced that sensation when someone we haven't spoken to for ages pops into our minds, and we get that feeling we should contact them. In empaths, this ability is particularly strong, and they can tell when people, no matter where on Earth they are or how long it's been since they spoke to them, need them. Empaths can just feel it whenever someone they care about is having a bad day, even when they aren't around. Some may even experience similar symptoms to that of the person they're "sensing." For instance, an empath may get headaches despite not getting them frequently if someone they're deeply connected to has a migraine.

- **Having an Impactful Presence**

When empaths are around, their presence can be felt. Empaths can use their energy in incredibly positive ways, such as healing others, when they learn to put their fears behind them. Loosening up emotionally and avoiding using their gifts wherever they feel drained and overwhelmed can be quite beneficial. Empaths are blessed with natural caretaking abilities. Remember how we mentioned that Mother Theresa was an empath? They are gifted with the ability to heal by just being present. This is perhaps because they can see right through facades and determine the uncommunicated feeling of those around them. Empaths can tune into the needs of others and adapt themselves and their attitude in a way that they could be of help. However, many empaths may not feel comfortable putting themselves out there, so they reveal this ability to those closest to them.

- **Heightened Creativity**

Empaths are very creative, which is why many of them, like Nicole Kidman and Oprah Winfrey, excel in artistic and inspirational fields. Empaths have the unique ability to delve deep into abstract concepts, like emotions, and come up with corresponding concrete ideas and solutions. Once empaths realize and unleash their creativity, they'll be able to make great things happen. Even those who end up working in analytical fields approach their careers with more innovative mindsets. Empaths may end up feeling unfulfilled if they find themselves trapped in environments where they have to conform to traditional ways of doing things.

- **Refining Your Powers**

Many empaths are born with potent abilities. This is especially the case for those destined to achieve greatness, just like the aforementioned influential figures. However, in most cases, empaths will need to develop and grow their abilities. They need to enhance and nourish their skills to turn into fully-fledged powers. While growth in an empaths' skills happens naturally, considering they'll learn more about the world and find their place within it, active development can allow them to use their skills to help themselves and those around them.

If you're hoping to refine your skills, the first thing you need to do is accept that you're an empath. If there's something you've learned while growing up, it's that you can't just turn your abilities and emotions off. Reading this book means that you've finally decided to embrace your nature and stop fighting it. Now that you've acknowledged your gifts, you can start channeling them for the good of the world.

Listening to your gut and following your instincts are also essential aspects of refining your empathetic abilities. As an empath, your instincts are almost always accurate. However, they're only worth something if you decide to listen to them. Spend time refining your intuition. You can practice meditation and use tools like crystals and essential oils to open your third eye chakra if you're into spirituality. You can also simply practice listening to your gut instinct even in the smallest situations throughout your day.

A lot of empaths struggle with their self-esteem. Besides growing up feeling insecure about their abilities, many empaths are easily drained and used by energy vampires. Changing how you think about yourself and knowing that you're worth it can help you realize and build your strength. There is nothing more powerful than a confident empath.

Since you're probably easily influenced by the energies of those around you, you need to protect yourself from negative individuals. Everyone has their bad days, and your ability to cater to the needs of those around you is what makes you special. However, some people constantly exude negative energy, hindering your equilibrium and peace of mind. This is why you need to set strong boundaries with harmful individuals and prioritize preserving your energy.

Part of being an empath is being a natural caretaker. Another huge trait's the dire need for some alone time. If you want to stay mentally, physically, and emotionally healthy, you need to be able to determine when you've had your fair share of giving for the day. You should make sure you have sufficient time to unwind and recharge from the day., whether this means indulging in self-care, sleeping, or participating in an activity that you like. Remember that you can't practice your abilities or help others out when you're drained.

Since changes in energy easily influence you, you need to practice seeing the silver lining. Negative things happen all the time. If your energy levels take a dive every time an unfortunate event takes place, you'll get exhausted. Since your empathy can't be turned off, you need to train yourself to see the glass half full of each situation. Changing your mindset takes a lot of time and effort. You also won't be able to maintain it all the time. However, working on it can help maintain your well-being.

Last but not least, you need to love yourself to nourish your skills. Compassion makes up a massive part of being an empath. So, here's food for thought: why do you show everyone compassion but yourself?

Why Being an Empath Is a Gift

Being an empath means that you're a natural healer. You are gifted with healing energy; you can communicate to others through your voice, hands, or even through a form of art. In fact, many empaths practice energy healing techniques because they believe they were destined to heal themselves and other people. Your heightened sensitivity isn't just internal; it extends to your other senses, allowing you to enjoy the aromas of beverages, flowers, food, and essential oils more than the average person. Empaths who further refine their sense of smell may smell diseases and deaths in people and animals. This is an ability that could save lives.

Empaths also have an enhanced intuition, or sixth sense, allowing them to sense potential dangers before they occur. While heightened senses and feelings mean you feel negative situations more intensely than others, you also get to experience greater highs. Many people would think that an empath's ability to feel so profoundly would make them somewhat prone to depression and anxiety. Although this is true in some cases, most empaths are highly enthusiastic. They approach life and its experiences with great joy and an inclination to be more caring, tolerant, compassionate, and understanding. These are precisely the traits that the world needs more of to be a better place.

Everyone in the world needs some alone time to unwind and relax from the pressures of the world. However, empaths particularly find comfort in being alone or spending time with themselves. Their heightened awareness and sensitivity make alone time crucial for regaining balance and de-stressing. If you're an empath, you may need your fair share of alone time to recover and re-energize, which as counter-intuitive as it sounds, is actually a good thing. Spending time alone allows them to be more self-aware, introspective, and reflective.

Empaths have a very creative approach to life, in general. Not only are they usually artistically gifted, but they can also think out of the box regarding scenarios, possibilities, solutions, and experiences. They have a different way of viewing things, which allows them to conceptualize things far higher than the average person.

Aside from being emotional themselves, empaths are great at reading emotional cues, making them sensitive to other people's feelings. They're great at sensing other people's emotional and physical needs without any form of verbal communication. This skill is beneficial for handling infants, animals, and plants.

Being extremely sensitive to the emotions and feelings of others makes them especially aware when they're being lied to. Do you know how people tend to say that they're fine when they really aren't? Empaths can see right through that. They can tell what's going on beneath the facade that people may put up.

Types of Empaths

There are numerous types of empaths, each of which links to the world in a unique way. While some traits are found in all empaths, each different type has heightened sensitivity and emotional reactions toward specific types of beings and situations. Many believe that there are six to eight types of empaths, at max. You may be surprised to learn that there's a total of 11 types. Some empaths are typically more powerful than other types. The Heyoka empath, for instance, is considered the most forceful. This is because they are highly spiritual, serve as emotional mirrors, and are thought to be able to read minds. If you're an empath, you may possess traits that trace you back to more than one type. However, the chances are that you'll display dominance in just one type.

The following are the 11 types of empaths:

1. Claircognizant Empath

Claircognizant empaths are also known as intuitive empaths. These individuals know what they need to do or how they need to act in certain situations, even when there is no solid reason or rationale behind these gut instincts. Besides being able to tell what they should or shouldn't do, these empaths can sense the energetic fields of others and can read people easily.

2. Psychometric Empath

These individuals can obtain information from the energy that photographs, places, or significant objects r significant emit.

3. Flora Empath

Flora empaths can communicate with plants. They use their energy to cater to their needs, allowing them to live and thrive.

4. Fauna Empath

Fauna empaths can communicate with animals and send them messages. This type of communication is typically initiated by the individual and not the animal.

5. Geomantic Empath

These empaths can receive signals and respond to signs from the earth or soil, which makes them particularly sensitive to natural disasters. They can tell that they will happen beforehand.

6. Telepathic Empath

These empaths use all their senses to determine other people's thoughts and feelings, even when they aren't verbally expressed.

7. Precognitive Empath

These individuals can feel certain events or situations before they occur. They may feel a wave of nervousness or anxiety as their intuition heightens.

8. Emotional Empath

These empaths can sense the emotions of others without obtaining background knowledge of the person's situation.

9. Physical Empath

Physical empaths can feel the pain and symptoms of others as if they were their own.

10. Medium/Psychic Empath

These types of empaths can see, hear, and communicate with spirits who have crossed over.

11. Heyoka Empath

As you know, this is the most powerful type of empath. They have an unconventional way of thinking and tend to mirror the emotions of others. They can foster emotional healing, among others.

Introverted vs. Extroverted Empaths

There are a lot of prevalent misconceptions about empaths. Most people believe that all empaths are introverts. While some empaths are introverted, many of them are extroverts. Like other people, each empath has their way of interacting and socializing with people. Introverted empaths have very low levels of tolerance when it comes to socializing. They typically despise small talk. Introverted empaths are also relatively quiet during social gatherings and may want to leave as early as possible. This is why they may prefer to show up with their own car. This way, they will not depend on others to get home. Introverted empaths prefer sticking to their small and close circle of friends, as this is where they feel most safe and comfortable. They shy away from parties and large gatherings. They often get overstimulated if they spend long periods surrounded by groups.

Extroverted empaths, on the other hand, are more interactive and verbal. Even though they're very sociable, they may be selective about their company. While they are open to outings, they often like to stick to the familiar and known territory. They also have unreliable energy levels. They may find it hard to decide whether they'd like to stay in or go out. Extroverted empaths are very open when it comes to their creativity. They even take pride in it.

Common Careers Adopted by Empaths

- Web developer
- Counselor
- Artist
- Veterinary technician
- Teacher
- Gardener
- Park ranger
- Graphic designer
- Librarian
- Editor
- Musician
- Social worker
- Professor
- Massage therapist
- Yoga instructor
- Therapist

- Dentist
- Business owner
- Nurse

Your heightened awareness, sensitivity, and empathy is a gift. It's not a curse or burden you need to conceal or switch off. Changing how you think about yourself can allow you to put your gifts to their best use. You will be able to use your empathy in ways that benefit you rather than drain you.

Chapter 3: Are You an Empath?

Envision this: You wake up, open your curtains, and let the sunshine through your window. "Today is a good day," you tell yourself and start getting ready for the day. You stop for coffee on your way to work and blast your favorite music in your ears. At this point, it feels like nothing can ruin your day. Everything is perfect until you run into a co-worker who's feeling under the weather, which of course, causes a huge shift in your emotions. Your good mood is long gone, and you feel just as blue as your friend. Does this sound familiar?

If you're an empath, you can feel the pain and experiences of others, just as if they were happening to you. This can make it challenging to provide your loved ones with the level of emotional support they need since you'll be trying to juggle the same emotions. As incredible as it's to be an empath, it comes with the inability to separate other people's feelings from your own.

We all have our own battles to fight that are both mentally and emotionally tiring; add to the mix being an empath, and it can feel like you're constantly fighting battles that aren't yours. Empaths get too caught up in the feelings and situations of others to the point of emotional exhaustion. This is also true for positive situations. While seemingly less burdensome than painful or sad events, extreme emotional stimulations can be a lot to handle, even if they're joyful and exciting. If you're an empath, you know you have a lifelong task of developing emotional management techniques and indulging in self-care. Otherwise, you'll be an anxious wreck.

If you're an extroverted empath, then the chances are that you're very familiar with the age-old question "should I go out or stay in?" Everyone feels torn between going out and taking the day off for themselves. However, for us empaths, it's different. We love connecting with others, but we fear that when our social battery runs out, we'll be quick to burn out. Being an empath means that you need some alone time to recharge, unwind, and process all your feelings and emotions. It's only fair after spending the day absorbing the pains, sadness, anger, excitement, worry, and fear of others. We know that if we are deprived of our fair share of alone time, we'll break down under pressure. Meanwhile, connecting with others can help us boost our mental health. It's a real struggle.

This brings us to our next point. If you're an empath, you're probably aware of the struggle that comes with people not understanding why alone time is a matter of life or death. Explaining why alone time is necessary is not always easy, especially when most people aren't informed as to what it means to be an empath – and how it is not the same as being a tad more compassionate, understanding, or sensitive than the average person to begin with. Besides, not all empaths are the same. Each individual uses this alone time for a unique purpose. For some, it's an opportunity to sift through the thoughts that revolve around in their heads. For others, it's when they work out which emotions belong to them and what they have absorbed from others. Some empaths simply use this time to reclaim their energy or strength, while others do it for all these reasons at once. Non-empaths don't need to spend as much time by themselves. Many of them also thrive in groups, which is why it can be hard to explain why an empath's alone time is that big of a deal.

Empaths need some time to adjust to the transition from low-stimulus to high-stimulus situations and environments and the other way around. This is perhaps why you may feel an odd sense of void after leaving large groups or parties or be extremely overwhelmed when making your way into a large crowd. Not everyone understands the need to take some time to process these staggering transitions and adjust to the strong waves of emotions that come with them.

Being an empath means so many things. It forgets to nourish yourself with the same amount of care, compassion, and understanding that you offer to others. It means that you find it hard not to go out of your way to help others, even if it compromises your own needs and well-being. It's also sensing negative emotions and instantly knowing that something is "off," even when no one else seems to notice. Being an empath can be extremely taxing, from being unable to withstand violence to being misunderstood and often taken advantage of. However, it's a gift that you wouldn't trade for the world if you took the time to understand.

It can be hard to determine whether you're an empath, especially when there's so much misconception about this "ability." The lack of education surrounding the topic, the frequent confusion between empaths and highly sensitive individuals, and the inaccurate labels and stereotypes can also leave you doubtful. However, reading this chapter can help you determine whether you really are an empath.

Life as an Empath

When you're an empath, you learn that constantly protecting yourself is vital. It becomes second nature the more you start to understand yourself and become increasingly self-aware. You may have never really grasped your heightened sensitivity toward some TV and movie genres or your inability to tolerate harsh news and stories. You may have found it odd that you would rather know as little information as possible on some significant issues or events.

Now that you know you may be an empath, it probably all makes more sense. The world and its dynamics can feel a bit too heavy sometimes. We, the empaths of the world, have to carry the weight of being upset by all the horrible events happening on planet Earth, from natural disasters to the incomprehensible deeds that other people do. You might not have thought much of it at first, considering that adverse events would naturally sadden most people. However, it may have come across as a shock to realize that others don't feel things as deeply as you do. Growing up, many empaths don't realize that not everyone feels overwhelmed and wholly drained when others are hurting. Child empaths aren't aware that profoundly feeling the pain of others isn't considered an ordinary aspect of the human experience. You are very likely an empath if you relate to all of this.

You've probably tried to switch off your empathy at one point or another in your lifetime. The inability to get over feelings that aren't even yours, or the struggle to turn your thoughts off for just a few seconds, can ignite a deep sense of frustration within you. This is especially the case when someone close to you is involved. Empaths can't stomach the thought of having someone they deeply care about get hurt. Those close to you don't even need to express their sadness and sorrows aloud. Your heightened intuition and sensations will make you feel their emotions. Our empathetic imagination may keep you up all night, thinking about your loved ones who are in trouble.

As upsetting as it sounds, you may need to distance yourself from some people, regardless of how much you love and care about them, to maintain your mental, emotional, physical, and spiritual well-being. Some individuals are self-destructive. They don't care to take steps forward to improve their lives and their mental well-being. Unfortunately, their turmoil is yours. You can't sit back and help or support them from afar, as your empathy gets you deeply involved in their issues. Even though they probably don't mean it, these people can drain all your energy.

Some children who grow up to learn to be empaths sense familial issues. They may cry for months on end, for no apparent reason (or so their parents believe), due to a negative atmosphere in their family. Although parents try their best to keep these things hidden from their children to ensure that they're alright, empaths can feel this energy.

Although it comes with inescapable hardships, being an empath also has numerous upsides. Even if you've always disliked your hypersensitivity, you must admit that you admire your heightened consideration, understanding, and compassion toward those around you. As an empath, you hate the idea of others experiencing pain, and you surely never want to be the cause of it. Your peacemaking, great listening, and natural caretaking abilities may also lead to your friends warming up to you. The fact that you're very expressive also makes you likable.

Think about it. You are a better person because of your empathetic gifts. You are the one who determines whether your empathy is a sign of weakness or strength. If you're always going to feel these emotions and have empathetic tendencies, it only makes sense to let them be your source of empowerment. Let your love, loyalty, tolerance, and compassion be what sets you apart from the world and drives you forward. As an empath, you probably seldom hurt others yet spend so much of your time overthinking and analyzing how you treat those around you. Many empaths worry about unintentionally hurting others, even when they have no reason to. Empaths do their best to treat everyone the way they'd like to be treated, making them special.

Typically, the most significant challenge comes from the inability to find balance. This is why many empaths end up withdrawing - in an emotional sense – completely from challenging situations, hoping to avoid negative stimuli. While protecting your energy is a must, you can't just evade life altogether. Embracing your sensitivity and understanding that self-protection does not equate to avoidance can help. You are strong enough to endure all your emotions and heightened senses, which is why you are undoubtedly strong enough to face life with all its negative and positive aspects.

Quiz: Am I an Empath?

At this point, you should be able to tell if you're an empath. However, we put together a short quiz to help you confirm your opinion. If you check off most of these statements, then you're probably an empath.

- People are generally very easily drawn to me.
- I can tell how my friends feel before they even tell me.
- I am highly intuitive.
- People trust me enough to come to me with their problems.
- I cry easily when watching videos, cartoons, commercials, or movies.
- I often feel drained after social interactions.
- I have been told that I'm a good listener.
- Physical touch can sometimes feel uncomfortable or invasive.
- I've been told that I'm way too sensitive.
- The emotions of others easily influence my emotions.
- I often cry in public.
- My emotions drive me.
- Self-care is a priority.
- I can sense the energy around me.
- I'm very easily distracted.
- I indulge in spiritual practices.
- I need alone time or practice rituals to feel grounded and centered.
- Emotional music and lyrics can throw me off.

- I feel anxious and drained at large gatherings or parties.
- I don't feel comfortable meeting strangers.
- I'm very picky when it comes to touching people or things.
- I consider myself thoughtful, caring, and loyal.
- I usually feel it when things are "off."
- I feel different or misunderstood among others.
- I need time to recharge.
- I've always been great at caring for plants.
- I feel my best when surrounded by nature.
- I can somehow communicate or connect with babies or animals.
- Babies or animals naturally trust me.
- I burn out very easily.
- I sometimes cry to release my emotions.
- I feel physically heavy when I'm experiencing emotional pain.
- The weather influences my mood.
- I go out of my way to avoid witnessing disturbing images.
- I'm artistically gifted in some way.

What Type of Empath Am I?

As you already know, there are a total of 11 types of empaths in the world. This is why you may resonate with some traits more than others. As we explained in the previous chapter, you may identify with more than one type. However, the chances are that you'll have a dominant empathetic type that you strongly relate to.

As you may recall, you are a claircognizant empath if high levels of intuitiveness characterize you. While all empaths are intuitive, claircognizants can particularly sense how they should behave or act in certain situations or feel inclined to make certain decisions for no apparent reasons. Precognitive empaths also have heightened intuitiveness, as they can feel some situations or events before they happen. If you're a psychometric empath, you are affected by the energies of particular places, objects, or photographs.

If you're the kind of empath who's mainly into nature, you may be a flora empath. Perhaps you've always had the unique ability to sense the energy of plants. If you feel especially connected to the earth and are sensitive to natural disasters, on the other hand, you may be a geomantic empath. If you checked off the boxes that have to do with babies and children, then you're likely a fauna empath.

Can you tell how others are feeling before they even speak to you? In that case, you are more than likely a telepathic empath. You may also be an emotional empath if you can tune into other people's energies. If you can feel other people's physical pains, you are a physical empath. Medium empaths can communicate with spirits from the spiritual realm, and heyoka empaths can promote healing and mirror the emotions of others.

It's also important to remember that not all empaths are introverted. If you're an extroverted empath, you may have a higher tolerance when it comes to crowded settings and social gatherings. However, you would still need some time off to recharge. If you're an introverted empath, social gatherings can drain you really quickly.

Feelings of compassion can feel like a heavy weight to carry at times. However, empaths are used to being labeled names such as "drama queen," "overly emotional," or too much to handle." However, others don't realize that their lack of compassion is what we, empaths, find odd and even frightening. With that said, it would be nice to take a break from the never-ending feelings of compassion. Having no control over this constant sympathy, compassion, and empathy can leave you carrying the burdens of the world. It often leaves us suffering horribly, which is why we can't help but feel responsible for salvaging the situation. Though, we must admit that our empathy is a gift. It makes us better people every day.

Chapter 4: Empaths vs. Highly Sensitive People

We've established that empaths are people with deep feelings. They can instantly connect with others and the surrounding environment, often mirroring the feelings they pick up. So, generally speaking, doesn't that make them more sensitive than those around them? The answer is a definite yes, but that brings us to another point. If empaths are *highly sensitive* people, then what about highly sensitive people? Are highly sensitive people (HSP) and empaths the same? Not exactly.

Empaths and HSPs share many similarities, but there are differences. This chapter will delve deeper into the differences and similarities of both types of personalities.

What Is a Highly Sensitive Person (HSP)?

You can figure out that HSPs are more sensitive than ordinary people, if just from the name. However, people's sensitivity conveys their inner reaction to external stimuli rather than mirroring the feelings of those around them, as empaths do.

Scientifically speaking, highly sensitive people, or HSPs, have a heightened central nervous system sensitivity to the stimuli they absorb from their surroundings. These stimuli aren't limited to other people's emotions. Rather, their central nervous system responds strongly to all physical, emotional, environmental, and social stimuli. From a scientific perspective, it can be called sensory processing sensitivity or SPS.

Those around them usually describe HSPs as "being overly sensitive" or "reacting too strongly." Although they're often disparaged for their "oversensitivity," their sensitive nature gives them a lot of advantages.

HSPs have been studied meticulously by Dr. Elaine Aron and her colleagues. Their research found that HSPs make up about 20% of the population. They were able to summarize the characteristics of HSPs in four key aspects, expressed by the acronym DOES. DOES refers to the following traits:

> • **Depth of Processing:** The ability to perceive and process information from their surroundings at a highly accurate speed. Despite that fact, they usually take a lot of time to make a decision since they need time to analyze information from every angle, study each course of action, and make a decision backed by reason.

- **Overstimulation:** Becoming overwhelmed by the amount of information they take in. Their sensory system perceives stimuli like sounds, smells, and touch to a much higher degree than non-HSPs, making them feel overwhelmed by everyday life.

- **Emotional Reactivity:** Reacting strongly to the stimuli they perceive and feel. "E" might also stand for empathy, which is the ability to feel others' emotions.

- **Sensing the Subtle:** Being able to notice and analyze subtle actions. Like a fine-tuned sensor, they're able to read another person's body language and understand their emotions from the way they talk or act.

How to Know If You're an HSP

There are a few ways to know if you're an empathetic person. Here, we've gathered a few questions to help you decide if you're indeed an HSP. Check out the statements that resonate with how you usually feel:

- You're easily overwhelmed by strong sensory stimuli - it can be a strong reaction to light, odor, touch, or any physical stimuli in general

- You always notice the subtle differences and details in your environment

- You're easily affected by how others feel

- You're very sensitive to pain and can't stand it

- You feel like you need to withdraw in crowded spaces or on busy days. You feel like you just need to go into a darkened room, jump into your bed, or enjoy some privacy to cool down the effects of being overly stimulated

- Drinking coffee or any other caffeinated beverage puts you on edge

- You have a rich and complex internal environment that you like to get lost in

- Loud noises make you uncomfortable

- You're deeply moved by art and music

- Sometimes, your nervous system is so overwhelmed that you need to withdraw and have some private time

- You are conscientious

- You get startled easily

- You get anxious when you have a lot of tasks to carry out in a short period of time

- You tend to notice when others are uncomfortable in their surroundings, and you know what to do to make them more physically comfortable

- You get annoyed when people ask you to do multiple things at once

- You try your best to avoid making mistakes or forgetting anything, even trivialities

- You can't stand watching violent movies or shows

- You become too stimulated and restless when there's a lot going on around you

- Whenever you feel hungry, you get strongly stimulated to the point that you become angry and lose focus

- You like routine, and any sudden changes rattle you up

- You notice the finer details and enjoy the delicacy of food, scents, sounds, or any form of art

- You do your best to create a comfortable atmosphere in which you can avoid getting upset or overly stimulated

- You're bothered by intense stimuli, such as crowded places, chaotic scenes, or loud noises

- You don't like it when others watch you while you're working. It makes you nervous, and you perform much worse than if you operate alone

- You were often told as a child that you are shy and sensitive

Your Score

If you've checked at least 14 or more of the statements above, then there are high chances you are a highly sensitive person. However, keep in mind that the results of any personality test only serve to help you better understand yourself. You should - by no means - base your life on it or use it as an excuse for a behavior you don't like.

Empaths vs. HSPs

Looking at the traits of an HSP, it's easy to confuse being an HSP with being an empath. Although there are a lot of similarities and overlaps, an HSP isn't necessarily an empath. Here are the similarities and differences between both personalities.

- **Similarities**

The truth is empaths are highly sensitive in nature. They share almost the same traits that HSPs have. Both types of personalities have a low threshold for stimulation; they need their alone time to recharge, are sensitive to physical stimuli in their surroundings, and have a limited threshold for enjoying their time in large groups. Both empaths and highly sensitive people love nature and enjoy quiet environments. They also like to help others and have a rich inner environment that they often get lost in.

- **Differences**

HSPs require more downtime to recover from the overstimulation of busy days and interacting with others when it comes to differences. Their ability to transition from a hectic atmosphere and connect with their quiet inner self takes more time than empaths. Most HSPs are introverted in nature, while empaths can be either introverted or extroverted.

Moreover, an empath experiences the sensitivity of an HSP on a much deeper level. Not only can they sense the subtle energy from their surrounding environment and people, but they also absorb it to the extent that they start mirroring what they've perceived. The ability to mirror their surroundings isn't something that HSPs have, and empaths unconsciously use this ability to enrich the experience they're feeling. As a result, they can feel what others feel so much that they may even exhibit the same physical symptoms. For instance, an empath can start blushing when they see someone embarrassed or get nauseous when another person has an upset stomach. The ability to mirror other people's physical reactions is known as somatic empathy, and that's something that only empaths can feel, unlike HSPs.

Moreover, empaths get lost in other people's emotions and thoughts to the extent that they may confuse them. They're often unable to discern their own experience from others, and you may notice that they start to act similar to the person they're with, and their behavior can change when they're with different people. Empaths are often highly intuitive and spiritual, while HSPs aren't necessarily so.

Generally speaking, an empath is probably an HSP, but not vice versa. If we consider empathy a spectrum, then empaths have the highest level of empathy, falling on the furthest right of the spectrum. HSPs lie right before them on the middle right, and ordinary people will have moderate levels of empathy in the middle of the spectrum. The further left you, you'll come across personalities with empath-deficient disorders, like narcissists, Machiavellians, psychopaths, and other antisocial personality disorders.

According to the categorization mentioned earlier, the empathetic spectrum will look like the following:

Empath-deficient personalities → Normal people → HSPs → Empaths.

What about Introversion and Shyness?

There's a common misconception that empathy and high sensitivity are the same as introversion. Although around 70% of HSPs and more than half the empaths are introverts, they're all different descriptions for personality traits. It's also not uncommon for people to describe introverts, empaths, and HSPs as shy, which is why we should make a clear distinction between all of them.

For starters, an introvert is a person who recharges their inner energy by being alone. Being surrounded by people or interacting with others for too long drains their energy, and so they feel the need to find privacy and unwind after a long day of consuming their energy. On the contrary, an extrovert enjoys social encounters and feels rejuvenated after connecting with others. This doesn't mean that introverts don't have friends or hate social events. They still find communicating with others meaningful, and they enjoy it. They just have a limited social battery that runs out faster than that of extroverts. As such, introverts get exhausted much faster than extroverts, seeking solitude to deal with the repercussions of socializing. This phenomenon is often described as an "introvert's hangover."

Introverts aren't necessarily insecure or lacking in self-confidence. They aren't necessarily overly conscious of how others see them or how they act in front of others. Instead, these are traits of a shy person – they're people who are scared of social judgment. Shy people think multiple times about how they'll look to others if they act a certain way, usually ending up hesitating and not acting at all to avoid making "fools of themselves," as they internally think. They also get nervous and start panicking when they're put on the spot or if they think there are too many people watching them. Their fear of social judgment leaves them frozen in place, even if they desire to connect with others and be at the center of attention.

When Empathy, High Sensitivity, and Introversion Overlap

Empaths and HSPs can be introverted and shy, or extroverted and self-confident. The way they turn out has more to do with their social upbringing and experience than being an innate or genetic feature when it comes to shyness. For instance, an HSP who grew up being criticized by teachers and parents as being "too sensitive" can become shy and start withdrawing more into themselves, all for fear of being judged. Here, their fear of judgment has turned into insecurity based on the negative feedback they got as a result of showing their true selves.

Meanwhile, an empath who is also highly sensitive may have grown up in a loving environment, surrounded by people who appreciate their empathetic and deeply feeling nature. They realize that they have a gift and try their best to share it with others without fear of judgment, so they don't become shy.

An HSP or an empath can be introverted or extroverted in either case. This part has more to do with their genetics, and their social upbringing could influence their introversion or extroversion.

The Opposites of an Empath, HSP, and Introvert Are...?

Let's start with an easy answer. It's obvious how extroverts are the opposite of introverts. Thanks to their ever-running social battery, extroverts enjoy a great deal of satisfaction from dealing with people, unlike introverts whose batteries get drained the more they deal with people. It's also worth mentioning that the opposite of shyness is confidence and charisma.

That said, identifying the opposite of empathy and high sensitivity is not so simple. At first glance, you may be tempted to say that narcissism is their definite opposite, but there's more to the story. Narcissists indeed have zero empathy - they're just incapable of feeling others' emotions or connecting to their personal experiences, unlike empaths and HSPs. However, just because they lack empathy doesn't automatically make them the opposite of empaths and HSPs.

An empath is someone with high levels of empathy, while an HSP is highly sensitive to their surrounding stimuli. However, people with little empathy can also be HSPs, and those with little sensitivity can be empaths. While empathy and high sensitivity have their good and bad points, a person who lacks these traits can also live a healthy life with their own gifts. They aren't necessarily narcissistic, selfish, or trample on others to achieve their goals – they're just normal people who exist in the middle of the empathetic spectrum.

We don't need to associate a person with a personality disorder because they lack empathy or sensitivity. Every personality has strengths and weaknesses. When you learn to overcome your weaknesses, you start to use your strengths and become the best version of yourself. That's a life-long struggle, but it's worth the effort.

Are You an Empath or an HSP?

Although empathy and high sensitivity can overlap, you can determine which personality type you are by understanding their differences. If you're still unsure about your personality type, here are a few questions to help you figure it out.

1. How Do You Perceive Your Surroundings?

To put it simply, an HSP is a person who is hyper-aware of all the little details surrounding them – they're able to see and feel more of their surroundings. Meanwhile, an empath is closer to having high levels of clairsentience that enable them to feel what others feel.

2. How Does Seeing Others Upset Make You Feel?

Both empaths and HSPs feel upset when they see others upset, distressed, or in pain, although their reasons may differ. An HSP is empathetic by nature, so seeing others distressed makes them feel troubled. However, an empath will feel what another person feels – their feelings and emotions of distress are a result of mirroring another's. They don't originate their feelings; they're easily affected by others' feelings.

3. Do You Feel like It's Your Responsibility to Take Care of Others?

An HSP will feel troubled when they see someone else in distress, and they will try to help them. Since they're hyper-aware of their surroundings, they'll instantly notice when someone feels cold or hot and offer to turn the AC up or down. Meanwhile, an empath looks for meaningful emotional connections with everyone. They also have a strong need to please others and take care of them. When they find someone troubled, they make it their mission to listen to their story, offer a supporting shoulder, and cheer them up as they search for their own answers.

4. Do You Easily Get Overwhelmed, Emotionally, or Physically?

Both empaths and HSPs get easily overwhelmed by their surroundings. They can experience both emotional and physical burnout, although to different degrees. While a highly sensitive person will get more overwhelmed by the physical, sensory, and emotional stimuli, an empath will likely feel overwhelmed by the emotional overload of mirroring others' emotions.

5. Do You Find Narcissists Irresistibly Attractive?

There's an inexplicable attraction that almost all empaths feel towards narcissists. We'll get into this more in a later chapter, but if you feel attracted to toxic personalities, especially narcissists, there's a high chance you are an empath.

Common Challenges Empaths and HSPs Face

Since empaths and HSPs share many similarities, there are also a few common challenges that both types of personalities can face. Here are a few of the daily struggles of both empaths and HSPs:

1. They're Easily Overstimulated

Both empaths and HSPs are easily overstimulated by their surroundings. An HSP's nervous system will go into overdrive due to external stimuli, while an empath's psychological system will get overloaded by emotions.

2. They're Quick to Experience Emotional and Physical Burnout

As a result of feeling too many emotions and sensory information, empaths and HSPs frequently suffer from emotional and physical burnout. As a result, they undergo periods of withdrawals and lethargy during which they lack the motivation to do anything.

3. They Tend to Become Isolated and Lonely

Dealing with others may be draining, but what really gets to both empaths and HSPs is realizing that they experience life differently than others. For people who thrive on making meaningful connections with like-minded individuals, finding that no one around relates to their experience is one of the worst things ever.

4. They Easily Absorb Others' Negativity

Empaths and HSPs are highly tuned to others' emotions and subtleties. As a result, they get affected by others' moods without even noticing. They might suddenly get moody, angry, or sad without any reason, although it's just because they failed to realize others' negativity has infected them.

5. They May Develop Anxiety

Being under too much stress for too long can result in only one thing: psychological fatigue. Once that settles in, it's common for both empaths and HSPs to start developing anxiety or other mental disorders.

At first glance, empaths and highly sensitive people may sound identical, but they aren't. While an empath's superpower is their ability to mirror other people's emotions, a highly sensitive person's superpower is their hyper-awareness of their surroundings and sharp processing ability. That said, HSPs have levels of empathy, although not to the extent to that of the empaths, and while not all HSPs are empaths, most empaths are HSPs.

Chapter 5: The Empath and the Self: Addictions

There's a social stigma surrounding addiction, as well as a common misconception that addicts are usually homeless street people or victims of domestic abuse or upheaval. People who become addicts are often victims of their own thoughts and emotions. Their disease may result from failing to deal with a traumatic situation or feeling so hopeless that the person seeks any kind of instant comfort and numbing agent – and what better than a drug to help them escape their misery? When you look at it from this perspective, you start to understand how empathetic people can be even more prone to addiction than others.

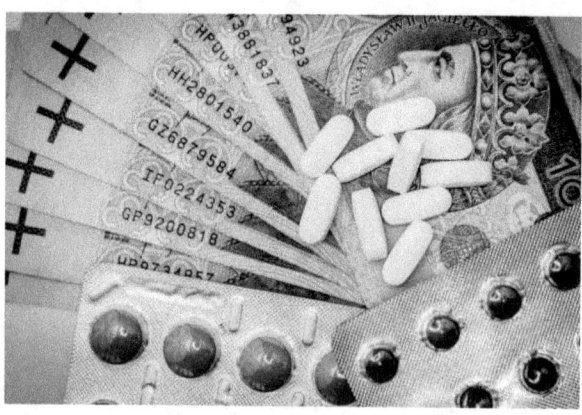

What Is Addiction?

Let's start with understanding addiction. A healthy human's brain is wired to react to pleasurable sensations by secreting dopamine - a chemical neurotransmitter that makes a person feel good. This neurotransmitter is often secreted when a person achieves something, feels proud, or experiences pleasurable sensations like having sex, winning money, or even eating a satisfying meal. To the brain, these experiences all "feel" the same, and so it secretes dopamine and makes its owner feel good.

The thing is, taking psychoactive drugs or engaging in addictive behavior, which we'll get into in a bit, triggers the same part of the brain that's responsible for pleasure. So, after getting a taste of this "high," the person starts craving it more. It doesn't help that repeated exposure to the addictive substance or behavior changes how the nerve cells in the prefrontal cortex - the part of the brain responsible for planning and executing tasks - works. These nerve cells become programmed to mistake liking the addictive substance or behavior to wanting it, hence the creation of the craving.

At this point, the dopamine secreted from using the addictive substance takes over the brain's reward system, and it makes the user feel there's nothing else that makes them feel as good as the substance of their addiction does. You'll realize how true that's when you learn that the brain becomes unable to secrete dopamine on its own, even if the user engages in an activity that previously felt rewarding, all because it's now relying on an external source to get triggered into secreting dopamine.

Types of Addiction

Until now, you may have thought that addiction is only limited to using hard drugs or abusing alcohol, but that's simply not the whole story. Addiction can take various forms, starting from using substances that can include more than drugs and alcohol to developing behavioral addiction. Here are a few types of addiction to help you get the full picture.

1. Substance Use Disorders

Addiction resulting from using drugs is medically referred to as substance use disorder or, more simply, addiction. It's divided into 10 categories according to the substance of use, although all 10 categories share the same symptoms of addiction. The abuser's brain depends on a substance to stimulate the reward and reinforcement system. The user develops compulsive behavior that forces them to keep using the drug at the expense of their normal ability to function. Most of these substances cause withdrawal symptoms when the user tries to quit, although to varying degrees.

Here's a quick overview of these categories:

2. Alcohol Use Disorder (Alcoholic)

Alcohol abuse is pretty common. After all, alcohol is available and legal to use. It's more commonly found in adult men, although the number of women abusing alcohol is rising. People can abuse alcohol due to its depressive effects on the brain, making them feel relaxed and forget their sorrows.

3. Caffeine Intoxication (Coffee Addict)

It may be weird to find out that caffeine can cause addiction as well, although it's true. Caffeine intoxication can cause insomnia, nervousness, restlessness, stomach disturbances, muscle spasms or twitching, irregular heartbeats, increased agitation, and fatigue.

4. Tobacco Use Disorder (Nicotine Addict)

Tobacco is a central nervous system stimulant. Smoking cigarettes or using any tobacco products, in general, can also cause addiction. According to research, 68% of adult smokers want to quit while 50% actually try to. Unfortunately, even if they do, they suffer from periods of intense cravings, mood disturbances, and lack of productivity, so most of them relapse.

5. Cannabis Use Disorder (Drug Addict)

Cannabis use disorder is more common among young people aged 18 to 29, unlike the previous disorders more prevalent in adults. Curiously, the prevalence of this disorder decreased with age.

6. Opioid Use Disorder (Heroin Addict)

Opioid use disorder refers to using hard drugs, like heroin, and prescription pain medications, like morphine. This addiction is most prevalent in those who have received opioid medication, after which they started using on their own. It's also sad to note that overdosing from opioid use is the most common cause of death in those younger than 50 years in the US.

7. Other Substance Use Disorders

We've only touched briefly upon the most common substance use disorders, but the list is much longer. Substance addiction can take many more forms, including using hallucinogens like phencyclidine, inhalants, sedative and hypnotics, stimulants, and other substances that alter the central nervous system and result in compulsive use.

8. Behavioral Addiction

Most people think that addiction is limited to using substances, but it can also result from engaging too much in addictive behavior. Here are some of the most common behavioral addictions.

9. Gambling

Gambling is one perfect example of how an activity can turn into an addiction. If you think about it rationally, you shouldn't engage in an activity in which you keep losing money, but that's just not how the mind of an addict works. Gambling provides an opportunity for an instant reward, namely money. This keeps the person fixated on trying to get this reward, often forgetting all about the negative consequences of the act. Those who fall victim to gambling can lose large sums of money, get bankrupted, and even lose important relationships, yet still crave the sense of reward that they never get. Gambling is now a recognized mental health disorder that also includes Gaming Disorder – or excessive video and digital gaming.

10. Food Eating Disorders

Even something as harmless as eating can develop into an addiction. Overeating and obesity have more to them than meets the eye – it's not merely the acts of someone who enjoys food too much. Most food eating disorders result from an underlying mental health cause, making them more of a symptom rather than a cause. Binge-eating is one of the most common eating disorders that cause obesity, but more types of eating disorders cause health hazards.

Some of these disorders are anorexia nervosa, periods of self-starvation, bulimia, which is eating and purging, pure starvation, and other eating disorders that include eating substances that aren't food.

11. Other Behavioral Addictions

It turns out addiction can result from overusing almost anything. Take excessive video gaming, for instance, which has been added to gambling use disorders. Other behavioral addictions can also result from the excessive use of things that trigger the brain reward system, such as overusing social media, watching pornography, going on shopping sprees, and other excessive behavioral patterns.

Why Are Empaths More Susceptible to Addiction?

Empaths almost always give off the vibes of warm and loving creatures. They'll always be the first to listen to others' problems and lend a supporting shoulder. They're the ones who try their hardest to make the surrounding environment warmer, be it their workplace, home, or social circles. They're too focused on making other people's lives better that they never show their own suffering, and that's why most people fail to realize that empaths are also struggling. In most cases, empaths are struggling even more than everyone else.

Being an empath means being an emotional sponge that gets dyed with other people's emotional colors. They become happy when others are happy, but they also absorb negative vibes at high speed, such as sadness, anger, and depression. That's all thanks to their hypersensitive central nervous system. When you review what we discussed about addiction, this is a scary recipe for disaster.

An empath becomes emotionally overwhelmed much easier than others. They also experience pleasure from their reward system to a terrifyingly heightened extent. When you couple the extreme lows with the extreme highs they go through, you can start to understand why they're more prone to addiction than others. An empath can engage in addictive behavior to escape from the overwhelming pain and suffering they feel as a result of absorbing others' negativity. Once they feel the euphoria of using substances or the pleasure from engaging in rewarding activities, they become much more easily hooked than others.

Keep in mind that being an empath is not a mental health disorder. We're only referring to the over-sensitivity of the empaths' brains that makes them more susceptible to becoming victims of addiction. For an empath, the initial phase of addictions starts with their need to dull their constant overstimulation. In their search for relief, they can turn to sex, food, shopping, gambling, alcohol, or drug abuse to escape from their pain.

Addiction is more common in naive empaths who are unaware of the negative consequences of their empathy. However, more self-aware empaths may still willingly start using substances or engaging in addictive behavior to numb the overstimulation. Unfortunately, both kinds of empaths soon realize how addiction is a costly price to pay for enjoying a brief escape.

The best thing an addiction can do is provide instant relief from overstimulation, but even that soon dulls as the substance of use or behavior stops working as it did in the beginning. When an empath gets back from their "high," they feel the effects of overstimulation far worse than they initially did. This can force them to increase the dose – which soon will stop working – and starts the vicious cycle. Meanwhile, their oversensitivity and inability to numb the pain can lead to depression, anxiety, fatigue, and more mental and physical issues.

Symptoms of Addiction

In order to diagnose someone with addiction, they need to display two of the following symptoms at least:

- They're using the substance or engaging in the activity for a longer period than they initially intended
- They tried to cut down, or have the desire to so, but failed
- They spend a lot of time trying to get the substance or engage in the behavior, and they need a lot of downtime following the activity to get back to normal
- They have a constant craving to use the substance or engage in the behavior when they're doing so
- Their use or behavior interferes with their ability to carry out their responsibilities
- They keep using the substance or engaging in the activity, even if that disrupts their social, professional, or personal relationships
- They stop participating in work, school, or social gatherings
- They may engage in the activity in risky places
- Despite realizing that the substance or behavior is causing psychological and physical problems, they continue using it
- They start increasing the amount of time spent on the activity since the same level doesn't work out for them anymore
- When they try to stop using, they start experiencing withdrawal effects - which can either be on a physical or psychological level

- They feel restless and paranoid when they're not using the substance or engaging in the behavior

- They always seek the substance or behavior to run away from their emotional distress

- They start to struggle with their financial situation, leading them to borrow money from others or even steal it.

Although checking only two symptoms can mean the person is struggling with addiction, the severity of the addiction is measured by the number of checked symptoms. Generally, checking 2 or 3 symptoms indicates mild addiction, while checking four to five indicates moderate addiction. If six or more symptoms are checked, this indicates severe addiction.

Self-Assessment

Not all addictions result from empathy, but empaths are more prone to addiction. Unfortunately, not all empaths are self-aware enough to realize the relation between their high sensitivity or overstimulation and their addictive patterns. If you're unsure about whether or not your overstimulation is feeding your addictive behavior, ask yourself the following questions:

- Do you constantly think to yourself that life would be so much better if you didn't use the substance/drink/overeat/engage in addictive behavior?

- Do you often feel the desire to quit?

- Have you tried quitting often but only lasted a short period and relapsed, perhaps stronger than before?

- Do you often engage in addictive behavior when you're overwhelmed by emotions, even if they're not your own?

- Do you often engage in addictive behavior when:

- You're feeling pain, anxious, depressed, or angry

- You're feeling hurt
- You're feeling uncomfortable
- You're unable to sleep
    - You feel insecure, criticized, rejected, or blamed
    - You feel emotionally threatened
    - You feel social anxiety
    - You're isolating yourself at home to avoid dealing with others
    - You're feeling drained, physically, mentally, or psychologically
    - You want to escape from the outside world

If you've checked one or more items in the previous list, that means you sometimes seek the comfort of addiction to cope with your hypersensitive nature. Checking four to five items means you may be suffering from moderate addiction, while checking more than six items can indicate that you're mainly turning to addiction to cope with your empathy.

How to Cope with Addiction

You shouldn't try to cope with the repercussions of your empathy through self-medication, which can so easily develop into an addiction. It's better to look for healthier ways to deal with your overstimulation while keeping your mind and body intact. Whether you're struggling with addiction or on the verge of falling over, here are a few helpful tips to get you started:

1. Be Honest with Yourself

The first thing you should know is that you're your own savior. There's no shame in admitting that you're struggling with a problem. It's the first step to getting your life back and living a healthier way, and no one will judge you. You don't have to admit it to others; merely becoming self-aware of your issues is a great first step to recovery and getting better.

2. Identify Your Addiction

Once you open the road to self-awareness, you'll start recognizing many behavioral patterns you may have overlooked before. Taking the previous self-assessment is a great way to identify your addictive tendencies and recognize your addiction. You may be struggling with one or more kinds of addiction, so be honest enough with yourself to identify any behavioral or substance use addictions.

3. Differentiate between an Addiction and a True Need

Sometimes, it can be hard to differentiate between craving something and needing it. There will also be times when you struggle with thoughts like "just doing it for five minutes won't harm." However, distinguishing between a need and an addiction, or a healthy behavior and an excessively addictive one, is crucial in your recovery. For instance, eating balanced and nutritious meals is healthy and essential, but overeating and binge-eating, even if you don't feel hungry, is not.

4. Accept That There Are No Shortcuts to Happiness

The truth is that there is no shortcut to happiness. Using a substance or engaging in addictive behavior won't make your troubles disappear; it only puts them on hold. It's even worse when you sober up and feel the weight of overstimulation crashing in. Instead of feeling everything all over again, isn't it better to take baby steps in solving one problem at a time?

5. Be Aware of Your Triggers

Did you know that even those who have successfully overcome their addiction can relapse in a moment of weakness? They don't even need to seek the substance on their own, but merely passing by a place or hanging out with old friends can be enough of a trigger for them to use it again. The same holds for you – if you keep constantly triggered by what makes you seek addictive behavior, you'll find it much harder to hold back or quit.

6. Limit and Vent Out Stress

It's important to understand how absorbing others' negativity affects you on every level. Although you're naturally programmed to absorb the negativity, you can rewire your brain to react differently. When others feel down, recognize how that will affect you and learn to differentiate their feelings from yours. One of the best ways to limit other people's effect on you is to set healthy boundaries and limits. It's best to limit the encounter with stressful situations if you can, but if not, then find healthy ways to vent out the stress you've absorbed.

7. Pick Up Healthy Habits

There's a long list of healthy habits that can help you destress. You should definitely start with working out, which will have the added benefit of giving you a healthier body and mind. Try your best to maintain a healthy relationship with food, and do not overindulge in smoking, alcohol, or other harmful habits.

8. Practice Self-Care

Remember to take care of yourself just like you're doing your best at taking care of others. Take a long hot bath, go to a spa, practice meditation, pick up a hobby that fills you with joy, travel somewhere nice. Treat yourself - you've certainly earned it!

9. Seek Support

Lastly, be honest and brave enough to know when you need help. Don't feel ashamed or guilty - there are countless therapists and support groups who will welcome you and help you get back on the right track.

For an empath, addiction is often the result of an underlying problem and not the main issue. It usually stems from the need to numb the effects of being overstimulated after becoming psychologically drained from giving to others. An empath is quick to feel and mirror others, making them an emotional sponge for negativity. In an effort to escape this overwhelming sensation, an empath may seek to self-medicate with drugs or engage in behaviors that turn into an addiction.

If any part of this chapter resonated with you, there's no shame in that, but you need to help yourself. While you're doing your best to avoid addictive behavior, take the time to dive into the main reasons why you need to escape. It's hard and can be very triggering, but you won't go anywhere unless you solve the root problem.

Chapter 6: The Working Empath

While empaths may face more challenges in the workplace than others, they bring many positive qualities to the work environment. It's important to learn how to deal with your colleagues and bosses as an empath or a highly sensitive person to avoid being emotionally drained all the time. If you think of your empathy as a source of strength, you will be able to channel it in a healthy way when faced with stressful situations at work. It's also important to find out the best careers that work for you as an empath and which ones to avoid. This chapter will discuss how empaths interact at the workplace, how they can cope with demanding bosses and tough situations at work, and what they should consider before taking a job.

How Empaths Interact in the Workplace

As an empath, you can sense people's underlying feelings in the workplace by a simple conversation or merely looking at their faces. You can understand and perceive their emotions, which allows you to make a huge impact in the workplace. If you meet a new person at work, you'll probably get a true sense of who they really are after only a short encounter. Your intuition guides you to understand how they can handle stressful situations at work, which allows you to get through to them.

You pick up on subtle signals seen in the way they dress, body language, and tone of speech, among other signs, and automatically process this information to get a sense of what they are like even beyond the working environment. You are not doing that to judge your colleagues, but it's just a tool that you have that helps you interact with others. This information tells you what they truly feel about their job and what interests them. You can tell how they might react in different situations at work or in their personal life. It's not that you assume certain things about them, but you have this inner compass of the underlying qualities of people.

Sometimes, you may have a bad feeling about someone or feel a certain vibe. Empaths are usually affected by other people's energies, and they can even manifest as a physical sensation. You may have experienced a tingling or numbing sensation when someone tells you a story about a chronic pain they have been feeling or an accident they had. You know how people say, "I get you" or "I feel your pain"? For you, that's completely true! You are actually able to feel other people's pain. Some people may give you such a strong vibe that you interpret as a warning signal to steer away from them. You can't explain what this feeling is, but you have learned to trust it over the years because often, you turn out to be right.

You can pick up on the vibes of any room you step into. You can spot who is excited or feeling down that day. You immediately pick up on everyone's emotions, and you use this information to make decisions at work or learn how to deal with a certain situation. Your presence in the workplace positively influences the people around you. Any business depends on its workforce, and when you are a person who anticipates the needs of each employee, your abilities can be a great asset. You can spot the weakest links in your company and produce solutions to fix these issues.

Many businesses are becoming more and more aware of the importance of showing empathy in the workplace. This is because they can see the difference between understanding people's behavior at work and merely giving them orders without assessing their needs. When people feel their managers truly care about them and their needs, they become more willing to do their jobs. This is why more companies are hiring empathetic people for managerial positions.

Empaths can recognize people's thoughts and feelings about their jobs. They can sense when somebody is not challenged enough or if they are overwhelmed. While there are some pointers like an employee's performance review, an empath knows that there is more to it than just numbers on a screen. An empath treats an employee as a human being. While it may seem obvious, not all people recognize the importance of people's feelings about their jobs. However, being an empathetic leader is tricky because you'll need to differentiate between someone who is truly going through a rough time and another who is faking it. Since an empath is unusually intuitive, they'll be able to spot that difference quite easily. These qualities make you a great choice for a team leader, a trainer, or a mentor.

Your intuition also helps you create strategies because you can anticipate what the company needs and know how to use people's skills to fill those needs. In addition, you understand the market and know how to think like the customer because you can put yourself in their shoes. For instance, you use this information to make informed decisions when planning a marketing campaign. Your ability to sense people's feelings and needs allows you to create strong bonds at work, not just between you and your coworkers but between them and each other as well. You can also anticipate problems that may happen in the future and take steps to prevent them from happening.

As an empathetic team leader or manager, you are often successful at promoting the emotional well-being of your employees. This is because you truly listen to people and not just implement changes you think are needed in the workplace. *You get your information from the employees themselves.* You may know how to anticipate their needs, but you don't just use this information to create a change without having a conversation with them. This process creates a sense of loyalty within your team and allows people to work with a passion and treat the workplace as their second home and not just a source of income. You know how to lead by example because you treat everyone with respect and trust.

Another great quality you possess is the ability to resolve a conflict. Your understanding of each person allows you to see through the disagreements between people. Being an empath does not merely mean you can understand the feelings of others, but it also means you can invoke empathy in them. You help them see the other perspective and not just focus on their own needs. You know that by doing this, everybody comes out a winner. This is how you create a harmonious work environment by making people more empathetic toward each other.

The success of any business depends majorly on people's problems and conflicts. They may need to resolve conflicts to collaborate on certain projects. You may need to approach customers to convince them to buy a certain product, or your business needs to pique consumers' interest to raise brand awareness. All of these are people-dependent processes, which makes empathy key to understanding what people really need. As an empath, you can create a strategy, manage a team, or lead a marketing campaign because you can easily tune in to people's innermost desires.

How to Cope with Demanding Bosses and Tough Work Situations

You could face tough situations in the workplace, like having a controlling or demanding boss. Your manager may constantly make you feel that you are not performing well. They may not support your professional growth or are taking the "tough love" approach because they think it yields better results. They could be gaslighting you by overlooking all of your accomplishments or undermining them. This is a problem that many empaths face, working with manipulative bosses who take credit for their work and make them feel unworthy.

Many companies go through several changes in their lifetime. You may have a supportive boss one day, and the next, you may be working with a toxic one. While this may make your work life a living hell, a few benefits come out of this situation. When you realize you deserve more than this bad treatment, you'll learn how to stand up for yourself. As an empath, you may try to avoid confrontations, especially when you know the other person won't understand or respect your feelings. It's important to look at this situation as a learning experience. You'll find out that being exposed to a toxic person destroys your self-esteem and can have a major impact on your mental and emotional wellbeing.

First, let's look at why some bosses are cruel or intolerant of their employees. Some people only feel validated when they make people feel powerless. They derive their power from stepping over people's feelings. When your boss is yelling at you to get a certain task done, it's not just that they are result-oriented. They need to feel that they have a higher status over you. They may have dealt with many toxic bosses before they reached their position, and now it's their time to order people around. They may think this is the only way to behave, or they may be under a lot of pressure from their bosses. In any case, they don't care about what other people feel. As an empath, you put people's feelings at the forefront because you only know how to lead with compassion. You know how to break the cycle of toxic bosses, and when you lead with love and compassion, you pass on these values to future bosses.

You should know that a controlling boss usually derives their attitude from underlying feelings of insecurity. They feel powerless and victimized by their previous bosses, which is why they feel insecure in the workplace. If they were self-confident or emotionally secure, they would trust themselves to have an effect on people and urge them to fulfill their job's responsibilities without undermining their abilities. They wouldn't need to bully people to get results. Bear in mind that they won't be aware of this issue. They may even genuinely think that this is a good way to manage a team.

When facing a controlling boss, you can become emotionally drained very quickly because you need a working space where you can breathe. You are already affected by everything around you and need your boss to be flexible and allow you to take intermittent breaks and not smother you with orders. When you take these breaks, your mind can process the tremendous amount of information you receive daily and create an appropriate response to each situation. This is how you perform your best work. If you are controlled and ordered all the time, you cannot work as efficiently. This is because you don't feel safe enough to explore your creativity in the workplace.

So, what if you are working under a demanding boss right now? What can you do to handle tough situations at work? Whenever you are in a toxic relationship of any kind, you need to set some healthy boundaries. Take a break from the surrounding negative energy to protect yourself and your emotions. You may be thinking, "How can I set boundaries with my boss whom I interact with every day?" Well, the first step is not to let their words affect you. While this may sound very difficult right now, it starts with a simple mantra: "I am not going to let his negativity affect me" or "These are not my feelings, but his feelings."

Whenever you have a bad experience with your boss, first take a deep breath. You can take a quick break to practice a breathing exercise and let go of any negative emotions. You can perform this exercise for just a minute while at your work desk. It may seem like a simple exercise, but it goes a long way to helping you move on from this encounter. Concentrate on your breathing patterns and then tell yourself, "I am in control of this moment. I am safe within my own skin. I will not allow his words to affect me."

Write down this experience in your journal. Try to identify your feelings and write them down. Mention how you wanted to react or wish they would have handled the situation. Create another narrative to that experience to allow yourself to heal from that encounter. It's important to keep this information to yourself. Be mindful of who you trust with your innermost desires and life goals.

You have to be very careful with whom you share your thoughts because you are prone to be influenced by other people's energies. Even if they were not empaths, many successful people don't share their goals with people who could be jealous of these ambitions. They may upset some people because they are not sharing these secrets. However, when you keep your feelings and desires a secret, you are more likely to achieve your life goals and not have the ideas stolen.

It's important to know how to know your value in the workplace. Chances are, if you are feeling unsatisfied or unfulfilled at work, your boss or your company does not understand your value. If your boss is controlling or keeps undermining your accomplishments, maybe it's time to look for another job where people will value you. In the meantime, don't let their feelings and emotions affect you.

You must know that a boss who is overly critical of your performance is probably their own worst critic. They do not value themselves, which is why they feel the need to undermine other people's achievements, especially their subordinates who can't do anything about it. Remember that when you were hired, your value was recognized. Even if your current boss doesn't give you enough credit, understand it's not about you. Your real challenge is to know your worth. Then you can decide between staying or leaving this toxic workplace.

What to Consider before Taking a Job

When it comes to picking a career, there isn't one rule that works for every type of empath. You could thrive in several careers depending on your passion. However, consider a few things before taking a job. The odds are that you will already be attracted to a job opportunity that allows you to interact with people and provide a meaningful service to them. Most empaths feel emotionally satisfied when they serve others. However, these jobs have a downside because you can become emotionally overwhelmed, which you need to watch out for. But, in any case, an empath is usually susceptible to being emotionally influenced when interacting with people. Some industries require an empath like nurses and teachers as they need to be sensitive and intuitive to connect with others.

If you consider working in the medical field, you must understand that it could be an emotionally taxing job. It may give you great satisfaction to take care of others, but you have to be well aware of its emotional consequences. This is why it's important to practice self-care daily to protect yourself. You can test a career by volunteering in a certain field or working as an intern to see if it fits you.

You'll need to find out if the work environment is a positive and safe space. You want to find a place where you can genuinely connect with people. When considering a job, look for the company culture and the job description to see if you will be able to communicate with others. Empaths thrive on having human connections regularly. You may be more suited for a job that involves collaborations than a job that only requires individual work. Take the time to research the company's values by reading its mission and value statements on its website. Some former employees will write their reviews about working in that company. All this information will give you a good idea of whether or not this company is a good fit.

Some jobs suitable for empathetic people are social workers, nurses, teachers, life or career coaches, writers, marketing managers, and UX researchers. Some jobs entail direct communication with people. Others, like writers, might involve working individually, but you'll need to dig deep into a topic and examine characters and stories from all angles. You will also need to think about your readers to communicate your ideas to them. In a way, you communicate with others through your words, whether you are writing ad content, web copy, or movie reviews.

While there is no limit to what job an empath can take, some roles may not be favorable. These include executive or managerial positions that entail making tough decisions that impact many employees, demanding sales positions, and anything related to politics, which can be incredibly stressful to any person, let alone an empath.

This chapter discussed the most prominent qualities in the working empath and how they deal in the workplace. We mentioned how to handle a controlling or demanding boss and the reasons behind their behavior. We mentioned a few things to keep in mind when choosing a job and company to work with. It's important to keep this in mind to ensure that you work in a place that values your abilities as an empath.

Chapter 7: Empaths in Love

While empaths thrive on emotional connection and relationships, at the same time, many of them struggle in these interactions. This is what makes self-care crucial to empaths. You need to learn how to recognize a toxic relationship because you might find yourself going into one totally naively. This chapter will discuss the various relationships in an empath's life and how to deal with the issues that come up in those relationships.

Why Do You Struggle in Relationships?

We can all send and receive energy to and from each other. Each person can interpret these energies and signals in their own unique way. As an empath, you are more sensitive to these energies than most people. This is because you can't help but absorb these energies and be affected by them. You can easily pick up other people's vibes and get emotionally immersed in their troubles. This makes any type of relationship hard on an empath, whether it's romantic, familial, friendly, or even professional.

You are highly sensitive to people's feelings and vibes and animals, nature, and even objects. You have a sense of a person's character from only a basic interaction. You can determine their emotional state by just being around them because you pick up their body language and the tone of their voice. This is the case with anyone you meet, even for a brief encounter. When it comes to getting close to someone, you open your heart to that person and receive their energy. Your own energy becomes attainable to the other person, which is what makes you so vulnerable. It's how you connect with others and merge with their energies.

When you are overly exposed to another person's energy field and emotions, especially in a romantic relationship, you are bound to be overwhelmed. This is called empath fatigue, where you absorb too many emotions and cannot process them all. They end up affecting you immensely, and sometimes you may confuse them for your own emotions. When you are emotionally overwhelmed, you are forced to take a step back from these relationships because you can't handle being near that person any longer. This is why most empaths find it difficult to stay in intimate relationships for a long time. As an empath, you need to have your own space to process your emotions and rejuvenate. On the other hand, some empaths can't distance themselves from emotionally draining relationships.

They become so invested in people's emotions and love to experience that connection.

Since empaths usually experience emotional fatigue and burnout in relationships, this can cause them to isolate themselves from people. This is a self-defense mechanism that they turn to when they feel emotionally depleted. As an empath, you may have distanced yourself from your family or friends because you can't handle the drama. You may have also broken up with a romantic partner because you could not have a moment for yourself. These behaviors may seem selfish to these people because they can't understand where you're coming from.

While empaths are intuitive about people's intentions and emotions, sometimes this intuition is clouded. This happens when they are intensely attracted to someone's energy or deeply invested in a person's emotions. In both these cases, empaths may still get an inner feeling that tells them to steer away from the person, but they choose not to listen to that feeling. This results in getting involved with toxic people like narcissists or manipulators.

These people are dangerous for an empath. They may be incredibly charming at first, but when they start to drain you emotionally, you are already too invested in the relationship to distance yourself from it. It becomes hard to listen to your inner voice because these manipulative partners know how to convince you of their perspective. You end up questioning yourself and believing what they are telling you. However, when you start to feel that your partner does not love you, you will start to withdraw or at least stick around until you have enough evidence against them. You may still want to believe that your relationship can be fixed, but once the trust is broken, you will start to listen to your instinct again.

As an empath, you often forgive people's mistakes and understand the reasons behind them. This can be extremely dangerous when you are dealing with toxic people. Whether it's a toxic partner, friend, family member, or boss, you may be subjected to emotional abuse over and over again if they take advantage of your compassion. You may even find that you attract people with emotional baggage or trauma because you are so well acquainted with emotional healing. You may be making excuses for people's mistakes and even share responsibility for what went wrong in these relationships. This is why many empaths experience anxiety and lack of self-confidence because people keep exploiting your emotions. You must remember that it's not your fault and learn how to spot these people and trust your instincts.

When you build any type of relationship on an unstable foundation, you will find yourself contributing to the relationship far more than the other person – this constant act of giving drains you. When you absorb your partner's negative emotions, the relationship starts to take on the characteristics of a codependent relationship. Suppose your partner constantly turns to you for approval or emotional validation. In that case, you may also depend on the satisfaction you feel when you are healing or fixing your partner's emotional wounds. This can make the relationship extremely complex, and it may bring you down emotionally to match your partner's energy.

You may be invested in a relationship by focusing only on your partner's needs at the expense of your own needs. You will go to great lengths to help them survive and overcome their problems, even if it takes a toll on your emotional wellbeing. This is another unhealthy relationship that empaths face. Your own compassion and empathy with other people's problems can be a double-edged sword. Your needs must be a priority because if you are emotionally drained, you can't give anything to people anyway.

As we know, empaths absorb other people's feelings. When you are in close contact with a person who is experiencing mood swings or anxiety, for instance, you will most likely experience those feelings. No matter how much you practice self-care or have become aware of this behavior, you can't help but soak up these emotions. This scenario is going to be particularly difficult to deal with, especially when it's coming from a close person. You may not absorb all their feelings, but you will definitely be affected by them.

Empaths usually absorb negative energies and transform them into positive ones because they know how to practice natural healing. However, if you are constantly exposed to this negativity, it becomes emotionally debilitating. When you feel loving emotions, you feel them so intensely that you think your heart cannot take them anymore. When you feel angry or down, this could affect your mood for days, and you may experience a general lack of motivation to do anything.

Empaths get emotionally invested in relationships very quickly and very intensely, so much so that you may lose these emotions as soon as you leave that person's energy field. Many people may accuse you of being selfish or heartless, but you may not even be aware of this. This is why part of practicing self-care is to be aware of how much influence you have on people's feelings as well.

How to Deal with Problems in Relationships

Now that we have discussed why you may struggle with relationships as an empath, it's time to talk about how you can deal with the most common problems. The first challenge is to work out whose feelings are in question and set boundaries. Many empaths battle to set healthy boundaries with people. Sometimes, you cannot differentiate whether your emotions are yours or belong to your partner. So, you should get yourself alone and work out what's going on. Take time to connect with your friends or participate in a hobby or activity that you enjoy. Then you can use this time to write about your emotions in your journal or practice mindful meditation. Distancing yourself from the intensity you are used to during the day can help you rebalance your energy and connect with yourself.

You have to find a balance between spending time alone and spending time with others. Sometimes, it could upset your partner when you favor your personal space and time too much. They may see you as distant or selfish because you don't want to spend time with them. It's important to communicate your feelings with your partner and listen to them as well. If your partner is not an empath, they may not understand why you need to spend so much time alone. This conversation can also be crucial to let them know that they can also enjoy their personal space to practice their favorite things. It's important to reach a middle ground where both of you can get what you need.

Another common relationship problem is that empaths don't know how to accept help from their partner. As an empath, you are used to being there for your partner, so it may feel uncomfortable when they are there for you. Bear in mind that it's normal to let your partner help you if you have experienced a problem at work, had a fight with a friend – or anything you face in life. When you are in a relationship with a loving and supportive person, allow them to be there for you.

As an empath, you can't help but be affected by other people's feelings. When it comes to your romantic relationships, this constant awareness of your partner's emotions can be emotionally draining to you and your partner. Your partner may have had a tough day at work and doesn't want to talk about it or is unwilling to take some personal time off to let go of some steam. You may not be aware that you are affected by your partner's mood shift. A good tip is to remind yourself to give your partner some space without being influenced by their mood shift. Take a mental step back from the situation and trust that they can deal with their emotions if they say so. When you practice this process several times, you will be able to let things be and trust your partner's ability to deal with their issues.

Sometimes, you may prioritize your partner's feelings and needs over your own. In an unbalanced relationship, you may find yourself always giving or trying to please your partner. In the process, you want them to be happy, but you find you can't talk about your own issues and emotions. This could lead you to try to keep the peace by any means, and you end up keeping quiet and not questioning your partner's decisions.

When your partner starts to exploit this dynamic, this behavior may lead to an unhealthy balance in the relationship. They become so used to being the center of attention in the relationship and neglect that you have needs too. This doesn't necessarily mean that your partner is abusive. It may mean that you need to assert yourself more and not be afraid to talk about your needs. In a healthy relationship, both your and your partner's feelings should be validated and respected. It's not a matter of picking a fight with your partner but about practicing speaking up about your emotions.

Start by having a conversation with your partner, as it helps to bring the issue to the forefront first. Try to discuss when both of you feel most overwhelmed so that you can understand what the other person is thinking. This conversation is often neglected after a heated fight. It helps to revisit the issue after both of you have calmed down. Suggest stopping an argument when a conversation gets too heated. Try to clarify what you mean and encourage your partner to do the same. Avoid interrupting each other when you talk so that you can listen to each other's feelings to the end. If you want, you can keep notes as your partner speaks so that you can respond to what they are saying when it's your turn. This encourages a mature conversation that can make your relationship a lot easier.

You will often feel that your partner doesn't understand where you're coming from, no matter how many conversations you have. You may have an understanding and supportive partner, but sometimes they just can't get why you are worked up about something. Let's say your partner made dinner plans to spend time with you. You could get worked up because you want to spend some time alone and may resent your partner because they didn't check with you first. Here, your partner intended to surprise you with their plans, but their timing was not right. Your partner may not understand because they don't ever feel the need to isolate themselves when they're having a bad day. They may want to get out of the house or do something fun. Both of your dynamics and responses to these situations are different, which is why they can't understand you at this moment.

When you feel that you can't communicate your emotions with your partner, it's best to create some space and revisit the issue later. This way, you will be giving yourself the space to process your feelings before talking about why you need to have some personal space. It's important to let your partner know that it's not about isolating yourself but taking some time off to recharge. When things get heated, you have to take a step back because you don't need to exhaust yourself even more. Just remember that your partner is allowed a slip-up every once in a while. They are trying their best to be there for you, and it's your job to make them understand your emotions. This only works in a healthy relationship, but if your partner is not willing to listen to you, it's a sign that they may not be right for you.

How to Stop Absorbing Emotions

By now, you have learned how empaths act as an emotional sponge, whether to their partner or other people in their lives. The empath in the relationship needs to learn how to stop absorbing emotions from others. First, you need to recognize whether the things you are feeling are your own. You may be unaware of the emotions you are carrying because of the story you listened to at work or a sad video you saw online. Many empaths find it therapeutic to keep a journal of their emotions, which they refer to whenever they feel overwhelmed.

In your journal, you can trace your steps for the day back to find out what it was that you saw or heard that set you off. When you write your feelings down on paper, they start to lose their intensity. What's more, you will be able to put a name to those feelings. When you name your feelings, you start to learn how to manage them. It's like a plan you have in writing to manage and control your emotions. It's also a way to know what caused you to be angry when you have been having a good day so far. Was it an angry coworker who has been having a rough day or a frustrated mother with her kids whom you saw on the street? If you can't find a reason for your anger, it's probably not yours but something you picked during the day.

Sometimes, you can sense picking up intense feelings from others. When you feel yourself becoming immersed, take a step back to the current moment and keep calm. Try to distance yourself physically from this intense situation. You can practice a breathing exercise in a separate room and remind yourself that these feelings are not yours. With enough time and practice, you will be able to observe intense situations as a bystander without being emotionally invested.

As we mentioned earlier, it's important to practice self-awareness and spend some time by yourself. Take this time to unwind and put all your feelings out in the open. This helps you become aware of your emotional triggers, making you better equipped to deal with them next time. One great tool to distance yourself from other people's emotions is to visualize a glass wall between them and you. You can see the other person's feelings without affecting you.

You can still distance yourself from other people's emotions and still be there for them. Since you pick up on people's vibes, you can listen to them and ask questions about how they are feeling. You will understand where their feelings are coming from while keeping your own feelings separate. This way, that person can share their emotions with you, which they will appreciate, and at the same time, you won't be affected by their turmoil.

In this chapter, we discussed why, as an empath, you struggle in different relationships and how you can deal with problems in a relationship. It's important to learn how to acknowledge your feelings and be there for others without being emotionally overwhelmed. Try to practice the tips mentioned in this chapter to maintain your mental and emotional wellbeing and find a good balance in your relationships.

Chapter 8: Parenting and Raising Empath Children

When you become a parent, you enter a new phase of life, unlike any other experience. Even if you have had pets, siblings, or you have seen children growing up in your household from infancy, having your own child is a completely different ball game. Even all your experience with babysitting your cousins is not going to help. Many people don't realize that hypersensitive persons - and those who can be classified as empaths - actually make extremely good parents. Because they are so hyper-aware of what is going on around them in their environment and other people, they have the key skills necessary to be good parents.

More importantly, they are extremely observant, which means they learn extremely quickly. As parents, they can observe their child, observe the child's reaction to certain stimuli, and learn what they need to do in different situations to calm the child t and create happiness, and it follows that the child will be much easier to deal with. Children, especially babies, don't enjoy crying, it's just the only way for the baby to communicate, and they are either saying they are hungry, uncomfortable, or that they want to go to sleep. The empathetic parent picks up on these things very well and can manage things smoothly.

The real problem is when you have a child that's an empathic baby, and you have a parent who isn't, or even worse, has a very poor sensitivity level and is on the other extreme of the spectrum. If the parents are on the insensitive side of the spectrum, it can be a recipe for disaster for both the baby and the parents. What is worse is that this problem is likely to only grow bigger as the child grows up, and the differences in the understanding of the parent and child increase.

Empathy is an emotion, a trait, a personality quirk, not a problem. This emotional predisposition should not be seen as a deficiency or a problem; rather, it's a gift and a unique ability that your child is blessed with. It's something that you should o develop and nurture. Don't turn it into a negative by blaming your child for it or suppressing it. Trying to suppress it or somehow extinguish it from their personality is an endeavor that will only backfire and have negative repercussions.

Signs of an Empathic Child

The first step towards creating a good environment at home and preparing the right circumstances for the child's upbringing is recognizing their unique traits and emotional and mental needs. Each child is different. Even two children categorized as empathic will have different needs, and this part of their personality will surface in different ways. These are some of the main things to look out for if you have an empathic child.

Different Social Needs

Generally, children enjoy being with children of a similar age, they enjoy spending endless hours playing and having fun, and they usually exhibit extreme forms of emotion. This is mainly because they are not aware of what is and is not socially acceptable. They are not yet disciplined to manage their time, behave impulsively, and haven't quite developed the habit of thinking before acting. They are spontaneous little people with a passion for everything. On the other hand, Empathic children tend to be more thoughtful.

For this reason, they don't always share the traits and passions of children their age. If your child is not comfortable with being with a large group of children, if they resist meeting new people, they just enjoy being at home and don't want to go out to play, don't look at this as a problem. They are empathic children, and they have very different social needs. This is partly because of their nature and partly because they are quite different at a physiological level. This difference is also exhibited in other ways.

Sensitivity

Children with a higher sense of empathy than average have different physiology to other children of the same age. Their sensitivity is part and parcel of their physiological makeup. Their senses, cognition, and emotions are all more sensitive than average. You might notice that your child is extremely responsive to certain sounds, they are quite picky about what they want to wear, they are uncomfortable in certain places, or they have a lot of favorites when it comes to clothes, food, spaces, and even people. This is because the things they classify as favorites offer their senses and minds the best kind of stimulation or the most comfort. They are easily disturbed by sudden sounds, smells, or even changes of plan. They can't help being extremely sensitive to these things; it's just part of who they are.

Interactions Have an Impact

Due to this sensitive nature, everything can have a lasting impact, especially interactions. As an adult, you might have come across people in your life who can recall nearly all the bad interactions they have had in life and the good ones, people who hold grudges for a very long time, and people who are extremely slow to forgive. These are also the same people who have very deep bonds, and they can be quite hard to access since they have a tough exterior. However, once you are in that circle of theirs, they are extremely colorful and uplifting personalities. These are empathic and sensitive people, and what you see in your child is the early stage of that behavior. This is why it's extremely important to help them understand how they should process emotions and manage their interactions.

Butterfingers with Emotions

Everything from physical stimuli to thoughts to emotions can deeply impact the empathic child. When something happens, i.e., they get startled, wear something that bugs them, or they just aren't comfortable in a certain space, their reaction can be quite extreme. Parents often interpret this as bad manners or think the child is spoiled, but in reality, that problem is bugging them so intensely that their reactions seem extreme to people who don't understand empathy. For the empathic child, the issue that someone else would brush off as minor is, in fact, a major concern and really upsets an empath. It's not that their emotions are out of place; it's that we think they should behave a certain way, and we can't understand why everything is such a big deal. Try and understand that what you think is an overreaction is just an appropriate response for them in their minds.

Compassion

Empathy is what these children are known for, but in reality, it's a general sense of extremely potent compassion that they feel. Whether that's someone else's happiness, anxiety, sadness, or victory, they can feel it like their own. They are so absorbed in the people they are in that they just can't help but feel the same way. An empathic child is the kind of person who will burst into tears if they see a random kid in their class crying. It's just how they are. These children will even love inanimate objects like their toys or just a door they really like in the house.

Intuitive

Not only are they intelligent, but they are also extremely intuitive. Few things take this child by surprise because somehow, they can forecast everything that comes their way. This can be a problem in some cases, especially when it's a negative event or something you just don't want them to know.

How to Give Their Empathic Nature Direction

One of the most important things you can do for your child is to help them manage their emotions. Children make decisions based on what they feel, not based on what they should do or what the right thing to do is, and this is even more important to empathic children who feel everything very intensely. As a parent, you are their role model, and these are some techniques you can use to put them on the right path and show them how they can tackle their own challenges in the right way.

Communicate

Children might be young, but that doesn't mean they can't understand things and get their head around what you think are complex problems for them. There are countless examples of children not yet ten years old and doing things many adults fail to do. Be open with them about the realities of life. Don't try to oversimplify things for them or mask the reality of the situation with a talk that completely changes what is really happening. In doing so, you will show them that it's ok to communicate clearly and truthfully. This will make your job as a parent much easier, and your children will also feel comfortable talking to you honestly as you do with them.

Guide Them through the Emotional Battles

Realize your child is going to face problems with their emotions. There will be times when they feel overwhelmed with emotions and start to act unusually, out of frustration, and times when it's going to test your nerves, but you need to be there for them. Using good communication and patience, you can work through these problems. These critical times are when they need you the most, and these are the moments where they will learn how they can handle problems. The way you deal with them will be the blueprint they use to deal with the issues in their heads on their own when they face a similar situation later on.

Role Model

Problems are a part of life; they are bound to happen sooner or later. Don't hide this from your children, rather present this as a case study for them. Let them be a part of your life and be a spectator to the events you are going through as an individual. This way, they can get a hands-on experience of how "adults" handle things, and they can learn more effective ways of handling matters in their own lives.

Manage Your Behavior

All of these things put a lot of pressure on you as a parent and many responsibilities on your shoulders. You need to look at how you act, deal with your own challenges, and how good a role model you really are. If you are struggling with personal problems such as addictions, anger problems, or just challenges with your spouse, you want to set a good example for your children and show them how they should deal with these situations. This is going to not only show them how they can handle those particular problems, but they will get an understanding of how they can tackle these intense and complex emotions.

Tips for Parenting

The main thing with being a role model for your children is to identify your child's needs and find a suitable solution. Each child is different, and when dealing with an empathic child, their needs are more sensitive. You need to pick up on what they need and address this as soon as possible and as efficiently as possible to help them develop properly. These are a few different things you should do with your child, and you can use each strategy with more or less volume depending on what your child needs.

Give Them Time

Empathic children are very connected to their surroundings, the people in their life, and just day-to-day activities. They are completely absorbed in whatever is going on, and this is one of the reasons why they prefer not to do too much because even a little bit of stimulation is a lot for them to process. You don't want to rush your child through anything, whether at school or play. Give them enough time to process things at their own speed. This can seem like they are taking forever, but they realize that they internalize things very differently and need enough time to take things at their own pace. Rushing them through things will only make it harder for them and harder for you since you have to deal with them after each episode.

Talk to Them about Their Nature

There is nothing to hide or be ashamed about regarding empathic kids. If anything, it's a big blessing for the child and the parent, and as a parent, you should be proud of it. It can be tough, but it's still a great trait to have in your kids. Let them know about it, let them know why they are the way they are, and discuss the idea with them. This will not only cut you some slack because they will understand why you behave the way you do, but it will also give them a fresh perspective on their life. Being the intuitive people they are, combined with their intense observation, they already know that they are not like most other children in their age group. Discussing the nature of the empathic person with them will help them put things into perspective.

Teach Them the Right Jargon

Teaching your child how to communicate more effectively is really important, especially with younger children. The basis of communication is the language, and the more you can help them develop their language, the better they will be able to voice their thoughts and ideas. Teach them words that help them describe how they feel, the thoughts they are experiencing, and how they can better communicate this information. This will make it a lot easier for them and simplify your life as you will better understand what is going on. When paired with an open communication environment, this is a fantastic place for both the child and the parent.

Give Them Space to Express Themselves

Sometimes it's ok to be wrong, be silly, and just make the good old mistakes that children make. As a parent, we all want our children to never get hurt, never have a bad day, and be the best they possibly can be, but they are human at the end of the day. If there is something that you don't particularly like – but your child really enjoys – let them do it and be free to express themselves. If they want to dress a certain way or explore something new, give them enough room to know that they can express themselves and be who they really are.

Manage Their Media Exposure

Empathic children, and children in general, are very impressionable. We are all influenced by the media, whether child or adult. This can be a real problem when you or your child spend several hours a day with the media. Whether this is in the form of a video game, movies, cartoons, or just internet browsing, there needs to be a limit to how much they can consume. Media is designed to keep you distracted and to keep you addicted for as long as possible. This can be extremely overwhelming for the empathic child, and even though they want to disconnect themselves from it, they can't. This is where you need to step in and try to make some changes that will help them regulate their media consumption.

Understand the Impact of Your Behavior

The significant people in a child's life are their siblings, parents, guardians, teachers, and any other person with whom they can develop a bond and interact frequently. The behavior of these people plays a big role in how the child internalizes different things and the worldview they form. While you can't do much about changing other people, you can definitely improve yourself and make sure that you project the best image of yourself in front of your child. Try to be the person you would like your child to be when they grow up.

No child care routine is complete without some measures to enforce discipline. The great thing about empathic children is that they are very receptive to your energy and emotions. If you are upset with them about something, you don't have to do a lot to let them know. They will probably already know something is wrong when you walk into the room. They are very good at sensing their environment and what's even better is that they actually understand you. You don't have to be excessively loud or harsh, just talking to them about the problem will get your message across.

Ideally, you want to start with something that will develop some rapport and some good energy before you move on to discussing the actual problem. This way, you can get them to actually hear you out rather than just block out whatever you say because they don't feel the right kind of energy coming from you. Also, try not to beat about the bush too much. Get straight to the point but do it respectfully. Try to build a conversation rather than just going on about what the kid did wrong and how bad it's. You want it to be a two-way thing rather than just a lecture they have to endure. Also, to make things less problematic, *set clear boundaries.* In every aspect of their life, they should know what they can and can't do, and when they cross that boundary, make sure you let them know and make no exceptions. Just one exception will teach them that there is a way out and that they can be spared. It's difficult, but sometimes you just have to put your foot down and get things straight.

With these tips and tricks, you will hopefully set them up for success in the long run and give them all the knowledge and tools they need to live happy and productive lives. Remember, all of this won't happen in a day; it's a lifelong process, so don't be in a hurry to get anywhere because it's the journey that counts.

Chapter 9: Empaths vs. Narcissists

We've touched briefly on narcissism before in chapter four, discussing how it lies on the far left of the empathetic spectrum. Briefly put, an empath has levels of empathy while a narcissist lacks any at all. However, that's not the end of the story. There's so much more to being an empath and a narcissist. Moreover, there's almost always an instant attraction between the two personalities whenever they meet, be it in a romantic relationship, work, or social gatherings. They say that opposites attract, but what happens when these two kinds of opposites attract each other? It becomes fatally toxic for the empath.

Let's take a couple of steps back and start from the beginning. What, exactly, defines a narcissist?

Who Are Narcissists?

Whenever there's a guy taking mirror selfies or a girl who posts six pictures on Instagram a day, and you get the impression that they like themselves a tad too much, chances are you could be witnessing a narcissist.

While it's true that all narcissists have an inflated sense of self-importance, there are more defining traits that diagnose a narcissist. Most of us have narcissistic tendencies that show now and then, but a true narcissist thinks of themselves as superior to others. All they care about is themselves, and they'll set out to achieve their goals and make themselves feel good, often at the expense of others. While they trample on others' feelings, intentionally or not, they feel no remorse whatsoever for those around them. More often than not, they don't even understand how they affect others negatively, so blaming others for feeling wronged by their actions is justified in their minds.

Narcissism is a personality trait. This means that not everyone who has narcissistic tendencies is a true narcissist. True narcissists are medically diagnosed with having a Narcissistic Personality Disorder, or NDP. People with low levels of narcissism will fall on the lower end of the spectrum, while those with pathological narcissism will rank the highest on the narcissistic spectrum.

Narcissistic Personality Disorder is recognized as an official personality disorder in the Diagnostic and Statistical Manual of Mental Disorders (DSM-5). According to the DSM-5, to diagnose a person with a Narcissistic Personality Disorder, they have to check at least five of the following nine official criteria for NDP:

1. They have a grandiose sense of self-importance.

2. They are preoccupied with fantasies about themselves, often dreaming about their brilliance, power, success, beauty, or perfect love.

3. They believe they're superior, unique, and special. They would only rather associate with others they perceive as special or high-ranking and get disgusted by those they perceive as inferior beings.

4. They have an insatiable need for admiration and appreciation.

5. They display a strong sense of self-entitlement.

6. They lack any kind of empathy.

7. They often exploit others to their advantage.

8. They may envy others or feel like others are always envious of them.

9. They're arrogant, and they don't hide it.

That said, a person can be a narcissist without making it too obvious. You may be dealing with a narcissist yet fail to spot them, making it often difficult to diagnose a person with narcissism without the help of a qualified expert.

Traits of a Narcissist

Let's discuss the traits of a narcissist in further depth. A narcissist will often display the following traits:

1. They Change Colors

At first encounter, you'll find a charming and charismatic person who may even inspire you. However, one of the hallmarks of narcissism is that they draw people in by their superficial charm. They won't show their toxicity right away, especially if they try to woo someone romantically.

2. They Have a Strong Sense of Entitlement

Narcissists believe they're superior to others, full-stop. As such, they expect others to treat them in a special way deserving of their self-image. They believe they deserve all that's good and are entitled to the best – rules just don't apply to them.

3. They Display Manipulative Behavior

Narcissists like to get what they want, and they often get it by manipulating others. At first, they'll use soft tactics to get you to their side and give them what they want, but they may change tactics if that doesn't work. However nice they may seem to you, they always prioritize their needs.

4. They're Thirsty for Admiration

Narcissists love praise and admiration. They already have an inflated sense of ego, but they can never get enough of being validated by others for what they take pride in. You'll often find them bragging about themselves and exaggerating their achievements, all while waiting for you to affirm their superiority.

5. They Lack Empathy

Narcissists don't know how others feel, and they don't care either. They don't have a drop of empathy, so they often disregard others' feelings, thoughts, and needs as trivial or non-existent. They may harm others by their indifferent behavior and blame them for feeling hurt or being too sensitive.

6. They're Arrogant

There's no one more arrogant than a narcissist. Not only do they think of themselves as superior, but they make sure you know it as well. That's why it's common for narcissists to be described as rude or even abusive when dealing with others. This shows especially when they deal with people they deem inferior, people who the narcissist will get nothing from by being good to them.

7. They're Selfish

At the core of every narcissistic behavior, you'll find pure selfishness. Whatever they do, it's always for themselves, regardless of any effect it might have on anyone else.

Types of Narcissism

Although many do, not all narcissists allow their personalities to be so obvious. That's because there are different types of narcissistic personalities, which have everything to do with how they were bought up, genetics, and personality traits. Here's a quick overview of four different kinds of narcissism.

- **Grandiose vs. Vulnerable Narcissism**

Both grandiose and vulnerable narcissists share a lot of similar traits, but the difference between both lies in their *childhood experiences.*

A grandiose narcissist is someone who grew up getting everything they desired. They have been treated as superior for as long as they can remember, and the expectation from society to keep treating them as such grew with them as they walked into adulthood. They're often aggressive, dominant, flamboyant, super confident, and exaggerate their importance.

Meanwhile, a vulnerable narcissist is someone who grew up suffering from childhood abuse or neglect. As a result, they have an internal conflict between their inflated sense of grandiosity and how they've been treated, making them much more sensitive than grandiose narcissists. Their narcissism serves as a shield that protects them from their feelings of inferiority or inadequacy. They're easily offended and often feel anxious about how others see them, especially if they don't receive special treatment.

- Overt vs. Covert Narcissism

Narcissists can also be overt or covert. The best way to describe both kinds is being extroverted and introverted. An overt narcissist likes to be at the center of attention wherever they go. You'll find them to be the loudest and most arrogant and insensitive people in a group. They go around fishing for compliments and thrive on attention.

Meanwhile, a covert narcissist is more on the quieter side. They still have the same sense of grandiose self-importance as overt narcissists, fantasizing about success and power. However, they're not as "loud" as the overt narcissists in getting what they want or seeking attention. That's why it's much more difficult to spot covert narcissism, especially when it comes to relationships.

The Fatal Attraction of an Empath and a Narcissist

Does it feel like narcissists are the exact opposite of empaths? In a sense, they are. That makes it even more curious to find empaths instantly attracted to them. It makes sense for a narcissist to be attracted to an empath. After all, there's nothing like an empath's loving and caring nature to feed their ego and boost their sense of self-importance. An empath is a perfect person to listen, appreciate, support, adore, and selflessly give their all to a narcissist, so of course, narcissists will love having an empath around. But how about empaths? Why would they be attracted to someone as selfish, unloving, demanding, self-entitled, arrogant, and insensitive as a narcissist?

This has to do with the empath's feeling of responsibility for taking care of others. Despite their endless giving and the narcissist's unchangeable character, they believe that if they love their partner enough, they're bound to change and reciprocate their feelings someday. It certainly doesn't help that a narcissist appears full of charm and charisma at the first encounter – they shower the empath with superficial love and care to the extent that an empath feels like they've instantly fallen in love. However, empaths aren't only attracted to narcissists in a romantic sense or vice versa. The fatal attraction between both can take on many forms, whether it's a romantic relationship, friendship, or even professional acquaintanceship.

How to Tell if Your Partner Is a Narcissist

Regardless of the setting, dealing with a narcissist is energy-consuming. You may struggle to put your finger on the exact cause of feeling drained all the time, but once you realize you're dealing with a narcissist, your feelings are bound to become clearer. Whether you're dealing with a narcissist in the workplace, relationship, friendship, or at home, here are a few signs that the person you're giving your all to is narcissistically toxic to you.

1. They Were Super Charming in the Beginning

The first thing you'll notice about a narcissist is how charming they are. If you're in a relationship with one, then there are high chances that your love story started as a fairy tale. They were constantly bombarding you with texts, they showered you with love during the dates, and they confessed their undying love to you so quickly. A narcissist in the workplace or in social settings is highly charismatic and goes around showering people with superficial praise. They maintain a good relationship with everyone without letting anyone get close to them. It's only after dealing with them for an extended period that their masks start to crack, showing their true narcissistic selves.

It's easier to spot a narcissist at home since they usually don't have to keep the facade with their family members. They expect their relatives to worship them unconditionally, and their arrogance shows in whatever they do.

2. They Always Talk about How Great They Are

Narcissists will always steer the conversation to themselves. If you're telling them about achievement, they'll be sure to tale the various battles they've fought and won. If you're complaining about an issue or looking for support, they'll whine about how their own life is difficult, yet how they're coping perfectly well with the challenges. They'll make you feel like you're less than them no matter what you say, always going into a comparison about how much better they're doing than you.

3. They're Always Fishing for Compliments from You

Despite their constant efforts to belittle you and what you're going through, they'll still wait for you to compliment them on everything they say and do. Although they appear super self-confident, they actually feed off the compliments to validate their self-importance. If you fail to meet their expectations, they'll somehow turn on you and start attacking your weaknesses.

4. They Don't Show Any Empathy

There's nothing worse than the feeling you feel when you seek support from a friend or a partner, only to find yourself talking to an ice-cold wall with no emotions. This is the feeling you'll always get whenever you seek support from the narcissist in your life. They're simply unable to feel your pain and emotions. Whenever you complain, they'll either talk about their worries or belittle your pain – often, they'll do both at once.

5. They Don't Have A Lot – *if Any* – Long-Term Friends

Despite their need for admiration, or perhaps because of it, narcissists only maintain superficial relationships. They don't let others get too close to them for fear of being found out. As a result, they'll feel envious of your close friends and get moody when you try to hang out with them. They'll lash out at you or throw underhanded comments about your friends to make you doubt them. This will either make you feel guilty for hanging out with your friends instead of the narcissist or affect your relationships with the rest of your close people.

6. They Constantly Pick on You

They'll start by teasing you, but after a while, you'll feel like their jokes are becoming too cruel, real, and malicious. After a while, you'll feel they're constantly attacking every little thing you do - from the way you eat to the way you dress, talk, laugh, or even sleep. They'll always brush it aside as a joke if you confront them and turn the tables on you for being "too sensitive."

7. They Often Gaslight You

Gaslighting is one of the hallmarks of narcissism. It's a form of emotional abuse that makes you doubt yourself and deepens your insecurities. Narcissists are champions at gaslighting - they'll insert a few lies among a truth, accuse others of false things, manipulate the facts ever so slightly to the extent that you start doubting your reality. A person who's fallen victim to gaslighting will start doubting their reality and their perception of facts, become less confident and insecure, start wondering if they really are too sensitive, feel they can do nothing right and that everything is their fault, and feel there's something wrong without being able to identify what it's. As a result, they'll start to apologize often, make excuses for the narcissist's behavior, and question their responses many times before giving them.

8. They Always Think They're Right, and Rarely Ever Apologize

There's one rule that all narcissists hold true: they're always right. If you contradict them or point out their mistakes, they'll come up with a thousand justifications for their behavior. If they don't have any, they'll beat around the bush and tell you you're being too mean. Meanwhile, they'll make sure to punish you for questioning them, either by ignoring, gaslighting, or being mean to you.

9. They're Hesitant to Define a Clear Relationship

You don't have to define every relationship, as long as it's mutually agreed upon. However, if your partner is already exhibiting symptoms of narcissism, you should consider it a red flag if they keep dancing around defining the relationship.

10. They Refuse to Accept a Breakup

If you get into a relationship with a narcissist, they'll expect to hold the reigns of the relationship. They'll never let you go as long as they still have a use for you. They'll be the ones to break it off when they get bored, and they'll never accept you breaking up with them. That's a decision for them to make, and you don't have the right to break up with such "perfect" beings as them. If you try to walk away, they'll lash out at you, blackmail you, and use every underhanded method they know to make you feel guilty and manipulate you into getting back with them.

How to Deal with a Narcissist

Dealing with a narcissist drains your mental and emotional energy, maybe even your physical health. If you realize you're dealing with a narcissist, you must take the necessary measures to protect yourself. Here are a few ways through which you can do that.

1. Realize What's Happening

The first step to protecting yourself from a narcissist is to realize the emotional abuse you're being subjected to in your relationship. Although it will be difficult for you as an empath to blame others, you really need to stand up for yourself and consider that whatever is happening might not be your fault.

2. Ask Others for Their Opinion

If you've been dealing with the narcissist for so long that you're starting to doubt yourself, you definitely need to get an outsider's perspective. Look for someone you can trust and ask for their opinion of different situations. This will help you build a clearer image of what's really going on.

3. Set Clear Boundaries in Your Relationship

Once you start realizing that you're stuck in a toxic relationship, it's time to take some protective measures. Setting boundaries against the narcissist in your life will take different forms depending on the kind of relationship. With parents, siblings, and partners, you'll be stuck face-to-face, for the most part, so defining clear boundaries to help you co-exist together is crucial for your well-being.

4. Remember Their True Nature

A narcissist will never change, no matter how much love and appreciation you give them. If you ever feel sorry for setting boundaries or trying to walk away, keep this in mind. They'll never love you or treat you the way you love and treat them.

5. Know When to Walk Away

If setting boundaries doesn't work and they refuse to change the way they treat you, it's time you put yourself first and walk away. It's going to be super challenging. They'll use their charm to pull you in once again, apologize and tell you they'll change, and go the extra mile to win you over. However, know that's all a game for them – once they get you back, they'll treat you worse than before as a punishment. So, walk away and don't look back; it's time you start focusing on your well-being, dreams, and future.

The story of the attraction between empaths and narcissists is as old as the hills. Narcissists thrive on the admiration they can receive from an empath, while an empath feels the need to take care of narcissists and fulfill their emptiness. The story goes on to show how every single relationship between a narcissist and an empath results in the same fatal fate: the narcissist thrives while the empath withers away.

Chapter 10: Understanding Your Feelings

Having empathy is a great gift that can help you build relationships in your personal and professional life. However, emotions can sometimes be overwhelming. Many people can be overwhelmed when they are extremely sad, stressed, or going through a traumatic experience. Now, imagine feeling your emotions *AND* everyone else's around you; how overwhelming will this be? This is what it feels like to be an empath. They are always feeling their and everyone else's emotions which can be extremely overwhelming and take a toll on their mental health.

Being an empath isn't always easy. No one wants to feel other people's emotions. Whether you are taking on someone's sadness or happiness, it can be overwhelming either way. An empath may not always be aware that their emotions aren't theirs, which is why they may not understand the sudden change in their temperament. Empaths don't feel their emotions like most people because their feelings are much greater and deeper. For this reason, they need to recognize when they are feeling overwhelmed, which will allow them to understand their own feelings and separate them from others.

Signs That an Empath Is Overwhelmed

Empaths are often guided by their intuition and are also very sensitive individuals. It's their sensitive nature that allows them to take on and absorb other people's emotions, couple this with a strong intuition and high sensitivity, and you have the greatest friends and partners. However, this gift comes at a price to the empath, who gets overwhelmed, drained, and confused about which feelings belong to them and which belong to the people around them.

You have probably felt the symptoms of being emotionally overwhelmed a few times in your life, but you can't understand why you are feeling this way. Being aware of these symptoms will help you step back from the person or situation that makes you overstressed, establish healthy boundaries, and practice self-care to protect your mental health.

- **Mood Swings**

    If you suddenly feel sad, lazy, or disinterested and haven't noticed anything that could have triggered these emotions, you are most likely overwhelmed by absorbing other people's energies. You can be happy and excited, and all of a sudden, you feel sad and anxious, or you can be calm and relaxed, and suddenly you feel angry and agitated.

These sudden changes in your mood are a sign of being emotionally overwhelmed. As mentioned, empaths mirror people's emotions, which helps them understand what those close to them are going through. However, you will need to step back when it starts affecting your mental health, and you start to suffer from severe mood swings.

- o **Panic Disorder**

A panic disorder or a panic attack is an unfortunate side effect of being a sensitive empath. Feeling different emotions all at once can be simply too much, leading to anxiety and panic attacks.

- o **Feeling Exhausted**

Constantly taking on other people's emotions and energies can make you feel drained and exhausted. When you feel someone's anger, grief, anxiety, fear, or suffering, you will start feeling tired. These emotions can stress your body and overtire your nervous system, and you won't even be aware of it. You will feel tired and exhausted all the time to the extent that you won't be able to keep your eyes open. Therefore, if you find yourself constantly fatigued for no apparent reason, then you have probably internalized other people's energies and emotions, and your body can't take it anymore.

- **Skin Problems**

It isn't just your body that suffers; all of these emotions will take a toll on your skin as well. Usually, various emotions can show on our skin; when exhausted, we get dark circles under our eyes, and stress can trigger acne. This has always been the case with skin and emotions; what is inside always appears outside. When you harbor so many emotions inside of you, especially negative ones, your body and mind will become overwhelmed and overstressed, and symptoms will manifest on your skin. You will start to suffer from hives, rashes, and breakouts. This is your skin telling you that something is wrong, and you need to pause and examine what is going on inside of you.

- **Mental Issues**

As you know, negative emotions can also seriously impact your mental health. We all go through hard times that can take a toll on our well-being. As an empath, you don't only feel your negative emotions, but you are absorbing and internalizing everyone else's too. So, mirroring emotions like fear, anger, or grief can cause you mental issues like anxiety or depression. In this case, an empath will want to find an easy way to numb the emotional pain they have been feeling to opt for unhealthy coping mechanisms like binge eating, heavy drinking, or substance abuse. They will go for anything that can ease their emotional pain and suffering. Most empaths aren't aware of why they feel that way; they just know that something isn't right and want to go back to their old selves.

Opting for unhealthy coping mechanisms can have severe consequences and can cause serious problems. Alcohol or drugs are merely a temporary escape, not a solution. Empathy isn't a disease that requires a cure. You simply need to find healthy coping mechanisms to protect you from feeling overwhelmed all of the time. Once you learn how to cope with being an empath, you will be able to use your gift to help yourself and others.

Healthy Coping Mechanisms

Absorbing other people's emotions is something that you can't control. Naturally, you don't want to spend your whole life feeling crushed by emotions that aren't even yours. For every problem, there is a solution. Having healthy coping mechanisms will help you deal with your emotional overwhelm.

- **Working Out**

    Working out is a great way to help you deal with emotional overwhelm since it will help take your mind off anything you feel or think of. Emotional overwhelm can make an empath feel stressed and anxious. As you probably know, working out isn't only beneficial to your physical health but also your mental health, as it can reduce your anxiety stress and improve your overall mood. There are various types of exercises that you can try, but the Autoregulation exercises will help reduce the panic and anxiety that can result from feeling emotionally overwhelmed. These exercises can also help calm your mind and body. They usually include meditation, breathing exercises, and muscle relaxation. Don't wait until you are stressed or anxious to practice these exercises but incorporate them into your daily routine to help prevent emotional overwhelm.

    If you don't have the time to go to the gym or work out every day, you can opt for short exercises that will make a huge difference. You can try exercises like jumping the rope for one minute, making 20 burpees, or 100 meters sprint.

- **Confront Your Emotions**

One of the biggest mistakes empaths make bottles their emotions up and refuse to acknowledge or talk about them. It isn't healthy to bury your feelings, and it can be so much worse when they are other people's emotions. Pushing down other people's negative energies and issues can have severe and serious consequences. Feelings can never be hidden or shoved down because they will always find a way to rise to the surface, and when they do, they will be strong and agonizing. Famous psychologist Sigmund Freud has done many studies about repressing thoughts and emotions and how they can affect your mental and physical health. Repressing your emotions can lead to high blood pressure, stress, and many other diseases. To protect your body and mind, you need to stop repressing the feelings you absorb from other people.

The easiest way to do that's to confront all of the negative emotions you have been absorbing. We understand this will not be easy, and you may be anxious or afraid of uncovering these feelings. However, working on getting strong mentally will help you face and deal with these feelings and emotions. Confronting them will allow you to learn so much about the people in your life: their fears, struggles, anxiety, and pain. You may come to learn a few disturbing things, too, when tackling these emotions. However, it's part of being a human; the good, the bad, and the very ugly.

We have discussed in a previous chapter how an empath needs to spend some time alone to recharge after having their energy drained from being around people and absorbing their energies. Spend some time alone or in meditation so you can process and comprehend all feelings, thoughts, and energies to which you've been subjected. When you fully understand all of these negative emotions and energies, you will be able to release and get rid of them easily.

- **Meditate**

If you want to be mentally strong to explore your emotions, you need to work on boosting your mental strength. Meditation has always been one of the best methods to improve your mental discipline, which is probably why it has been practiced for centuries, and its popularity hasn't died down. As an empath, making meditation a part of your lifestyle can have a positive impact. Meditation will give you the chance to focus on the present moment and help you clear your mind and be alone with your thoughts. Practicing meditation every day will also help you get rid of all the emotions you have been absorbing all day.

Meditation is easy, and if you are new to it, you will find many guided sessions online. However, the premise is pretty much the same. You need to sit comfortably in a quiet spot with no distractions, try to be present and focused on the here and now, don't think about the past or worry about the future or things that aren't real or may never happen. Be focused on this moment; it's all you have. That said, some thoughts or worries may creep in while meditating. Don't try to fight them or let them interfere with your meditation. Just imagine that they are clouds, and you are watching them passing by. Don't give them any attention.

In addition to meditation, spending some time alone can also help you manage emotional overwhelm. As mentioned, being around people can drain an empath and cause emotional overwhelm. Therefore, if you spend a couple of hours every day alone in a quiet room, you will be able to manage your feelings and energy. Additionally, you should also try breathing exercises to calm yourself down. It's very easy, and you can do them anywhere. Just take a deep breath through your nose and release it through your mouth. Like meditation, you also need to focus on this very moment. Forget the world around you and only focus on your breathing.

- Express Yourself Through Art

Art has always been a great outlet for people to express themselves and get rid of their negative emotions. If an empath wants to cope with emotional overwhelm, they need to tap into their creative side. There are various types of art that you can try, like painting, writing, singing, acting, and many more. Find something that you enjoy or are good at, and go for it; whatever form of art that you choose will help you release all of the negative emotions that have been consuming you for so long.

Art is very relaxing and can help reduce stress for anyone, not just empaths. Just like exercise and meditation, art can help you clear your mind. This is because art will help you stay focused on the task you are working on, so you will not be concerned with anything else. For instance, if you are writing or painting, you will only be focused on the project at hand and feel a sense of calmness and relaxation because you are creating something.

This coping mechanism can help you understand your emotions. For example, when you put what you are feeling on paper, you will give yourself the chance to understand these emotions better as they will be clear to you, and you won't have to wonder about your feelings. Additionally, art can help you express yourself. Maybe one day you can be a famous artist or writer. Sensitive souls like you can excel in these careers.

Many studies have shown the positive impact of art on people who have suffered trauma in their lives.

Understandably, empaths aren't traumatized individuals, but they exhibit similar symptoms. These studies have shown that art can reduce depression in traumatized adults, proving that it can help empaths cope and manage emotional overwhelm.

- **You Can't Help Everyone**

Although empaths are gifted individuals, they aren't superheroes. They may seem like it, though, since they can understand exactly what someone is thinking and feel the emotions of the people around them. It's a unique ability indeed, but what exactly do empaths do with this ability? Empaths are always aware of the pain and struggle the people around them are going through. Your compassionate and sensitive nature will make you feel responsible for them and that you need to act fast to help them out. Additionally, you probably believe deep down that if you help these people, they will feel better, and, in turn, you will also feel better and get rid of all of the negative emotions that have taken over your heart and mind. In other words, if you make a miserable person feel happy, an angry person feels calm, or make someone scared feel safe, then there will be no negative emotions for you to absorb, and you will feel better as well.

However, you aren't a superhero, and you can't save everyone or fix their problems. You can't just walk down the street, feel someone's pain, and offer to help. Although it's a sweet thought, it's unrealistic. Just as you need to separate your emotions from other people's, you need to accept that other people's problems aren't your responsibility to solve or your burden to carry. This can damage your mental health. If you allow yourself to be concerned with everyone else's problems and try to produce solutions, then you will not have any time or energy for your problems or well-being. You will neglect yourself and your needs for the sake of others, and eventually, you will burn yourself out and won't be able to help anyone, including yourself. The key here is to find balance. Help others only when you can, and you shouldn't let it interfere with your well-being. There are also times when you will have to put yourself first, which is ok. There is nothing selfish about that, even if some people try to take advantage of your sensitive nature to convince you otherwise.

For instance, if a friend is asking you to drive them to the airport and you have an important meeting, you can't just drop everything for them. As mentioned in previous chapters, you need to say no without feeling guilty and set boundaries. Your friend can simply ask someone else or call an Uber, but they shouldn't expect you to ignore an important meeting when they can easily find other options. Another thing that you need to understand is that you can't save everyone. An empath may feel disappointed if they fail to help someone. For instance, if you have a friend who is an addict and you are trying to help them get into rehab and get clean, but they refuse, you can't feel bad or guilty about it. Normally, you don't want to see your friend suffer and want to save them. However, you need to understand that you can't help someone who doesn't want or accept your help, and you can't save people from themselves. You need to stop carrying the world's burdens on your shoulders. You aren't Superman.

You have a gift, and if you learn how to use it, it can change your life for the better. However, to take advantage of your abilities, you first need to understand your feelings and know when overwhelmed. Once you recognize the symptoms of being emotionally overwhelmed, you can try any coping mechanisms mentioned here to help you manage these feelings. Incorporate these mechanisms in your lifestyle and daily routine to help prevent feeling overwhelmed before it happens.

Chapter 11: Setting Boundaries

Relationships with friends, family, coworkers, and even just strangers you come across in life need to be managed in a way that benefits you both. We often interact without paying attention to how this interaction impacts the other person or us. We go by routine, by intuition, and we follow a form of communication and interaction that we have developed, without much thought over why we have developed it that way or what functional purpose it serves. This is especially true for people with a higher sensitivity since all of these interactions have a much deeper impact on empaths.

Interactions as an Empath

We all feel emotions, we all feel things like empathy and compassion, but these feelings are far more intense when it comes to the empath. An empath will feel like even the smallest interaction has had a profound impact. Just a small problem with a friend, a little scrap with a coworker will send the empath down a thought rabbit hole, where they start analyzing things at a much deeper level than necessary. There is no need to look into things in so much detail, but the empath cannot help him or herself. Similarly, if they feel a good emotion from some interaction, they will often take it out of proportion again, which can lead to thinking too much, leading to all kinds of challenges down the road.

For instance, if they have a good conversation with someone, an empath will expand on this interaction thinking about how great that person was, how they must be wonderful in all aspects of their life and will think it will be a good idea to get to know them a bit more. In reality, this could be very far from the truth. Just one interaction, or even a few interactions, doesn't mean a person is completely good or completely bad.

All these interactions impact the mental and emotional health of the empath. Continuing to think about things in such an unnecessarily deep manner is both a cumbersome process and one that doesn't always lead to good results. This is why having boundaries in relationships is very important. Even if personal relationships are between siblings, parents, or your significant other, having some boundary line is always beneficial.

It's important to set boundaries and detect boundaries that others have placed and respect the space they want to have. As empaths feel everything so intensely, it's very difficult for them to stop themselves and resist the urge to become emotionally attached to someone. In reality, the person might not be comfortable with this, which could lead to all kinds of uncomfortable situations.

Types of Boundaries

The right kinds of boundaries help us manage our relationships better, and for empaths, this means it also helps to regulate their emotions and the way they think. Without a good boundary setup, it can be very easy to waste energy and emotions on things that really don't need it and not provide enough to things that do need more energy and emotional input. Here are the main kinds of boundaries that are used in social life.

- **Physical**

This is the one you might have felt most in your life and even found problematic. As humans, we want to have our "personal space." This is not about having your own home or your own room but literally just having enough space around you when you are in an interaction. Even before social distancing was a thing, it was generally considered bad manners to stand too close to a person if you were waiting in line with them or being too close to someone when you are sitting at the dinner table.

This relates to the physical space that we have around us. Generally, when it's someone that you are comfortable with, you won't mind them being really close to you; you might not even mind them having their arm around your neck. With people you don't know that well, you will want more space, ideally at least two or three feet away. With people who are complete strangers, you will want at least four or more feet of space from them.

- **Sexual**

Related to physical boundaries, one that's more about the personal relationships that we have are the sexual boundaries that we like to have. For instance, for some people having a kiss in public or just having any kind of public display of affection is a serious problem. It makes them extremely uncomfortable and can really upset them. For others, holding hands and other displays of affection don't affect them at all. In fact, not having public displays of affection from their partner can even make them angry. Similarly, different people want their relationships to advance at different speeds. Everyone has their own unique ways of dealing with intimacy, so it's best to give people as much space as you can in this regard.

- **Mental**

Mental boundaries can also be classified as intellectual boundaries generally. When you don't "get along" with someone, you want to have a bit more space between you and that person. When you meet someone who thinks like you, or at least you feel like you have a mental connection, you don't mind them being that close to you. Similarly, when you have that connection with someone, it's not just about physical proximity, but that person is close to you in your mind; they naturally just have a higher ranking in your mind when you think about them. This is also about how open you are about expressing yourself and the extent to which you actually share your real thoughts and ideas with people. When you feel mentally connected to them, you also tend to have a level of trust, which really changes the relationship's dynamic.

- **Emotional**

Emotional boundaries have to do with how we process things that we go through in life and specifically the interactions we experience. Emotional boundaries are tied to all the other kinds of boundaries we have painstakingly put in place. Generally, when a physical, mental, or other boundary is crossed, this also impacts how we feel. Similarly, different people also have a natural disposition as to how open or closed they are emotional. This influences how emotionally attached they are in certain situations. Empaths tend to have very open emotional boundaries, and this is the unique trait of empaths which can be good or bad, depending on the situation.

What Boundaries Are

When we think of setting up boundaries, it helps to know what exactly these boundaries are for, the kind of benefits we are looking to achieve from having these boundaries, and how they can benefit other people in our life. For empaths, on the plus side is that they help to restore self-respect. Empaths often get dragged into so many different relationships and roles so easily that they forget that they are unique individuals. They start to feel like a doormat that exists only to fulfill the social needs of others and should not have any personal requirements from the relationships they are in. Every relationship is a two-way street. As an empath, you have just as much right to expect something from that relationship as the other person who expects you to always be there.

Boundaries are a way for us to define what we are and what we aren't. For empaths, especially, it can get really overwhelming and confusing to be in so many different roles simultaneously. As you develop your ability to set boundaries and create limits on interactions, you are essentially working on yourself and improving the quality of the relationship. Rather than wasting yourself on every person you come across, you should focus on a few interactions and make them as high quality as possible.

This will give you more control over how you lead your life and give you more freedom to live as you desire rather than under the pressure of the relationships you foster. Also, look at boundaries as a way of respecting the people around you. You are not just being present there for the sake of it, but rather you are there to give them the very best of you.

What Boundaries Are Not

At the same time, you should also know how to effectively use boundaries and not use this as an excuse to save yourself from certain people or interactions. Having boundaries around you doesn't mean that you are isolating yourself from life or ignoring people in your life. It's simply that you are optimizing your social life, which will benefit everyone. However, if you feel like you just don't want to be around someone where you don't feel comfortable, there is no harm in drawing a line there creating some space. Similarly, you should impose these boundaries in such a way that it doesn't offend people, nor do they feel like you are trying to push them away. After all, they are still a part of your life, but you just want things to be a bit more streamlined.

Having boundaries doesn't mean you are selfish; it means you know what is right for you and what your priorities are, and you are focusing on your life. As an empath, it's in your nature to be overly concerned about people, and if you realize this isn't the best way to deal with things, then boundaries will help you. Again, this doesn't mean you suddenly don't care, but you are certainly not concerned with things that are none of your business. It's all about giving yourself direction in your interactions and improving the quality of life by focusing your energy on a specific direction.

How to Set Boundaries

At this point, you have already spent several years living as an empath. The people around you perceive you a certain way, and you are probably accustomed to living in a certain way. The way you behave in social settings the way you interact with people are all things that are going to go through a slight change when you start to change the way you set boundaries for yourself. While it might seem like a difficult task, it can be done and will be beneficial in the long run. Here are a few techniques you can adopt.

- **Understand Your Requirements**

The first exercise is to self-evaluate and understand your requirements, what makes you happy and what doesn't. You can start off with a pen and paper and note down what really makes you uncomfortable in your current social relationships. In this exercise, you can cover all your relationships and even think of hypothetical examples. As you know how you would react in any given situation, you can hypothesize how you would behave in a given situation if it were to come up, such as meeting a new boss, having an interview, or meeting someone new through a friend.

In this way, you'll develop a list of all the things you want, the things you like, and a list of things you prefer in your social interactions. From here, you can start to examine what you need to change and how you can go about it. You might find that you are fine with how you interact with new people and those that are not very close to you, but you aren't happy with how you deal with your very private relationships. This will be the blueprint for changing your interactions and what areas you want to focus on. From here, you can implement the following techniques to achieve the desired results.

- **Learn to Say No**

If there is one word an empath doesn't have in their dictionary, it's "no," and yet this is the most powerful word to use to build boundaries and good relationships. One of the biggest challenges for the empath is they get dragged into situations, or they push themselves into situations they don't want to be a part of in the first place. And so, the starts the process of living in uncomfortable situations, difficult to get out of, once you're in it. On the other side of the coin, when the empath cannot say no to themselves and cannot push themselves into the direction that they really want to go in, they are left regretting making the wrong decisions. Just by saying no, either to themselves or to other people, the empath can build the boundary that they need to safeguard their interests and the interests of others. Saying no will be difficult by trying to do it with the small things and build up the capacity to say no to the big things too.

o **Stand Up for Yourself**

Realize what it's that really makes you happy, what you prefer, and where you really want to go with your life. As an empath, you are constantly swayed by emotions that don't belong to you, and it's easy to lose track of what you really want to do. The ability to stand up for yourself goes hand in hand with the ability to say no to the things that you don't want and to say yes to the things that you do want as the empath is so preoccupied with other activities and other commitments, they often unwillingly have to forgo the things they really want. Creating boundaries will help you create the time and energy you need to stand up for yourself and pursue your own dreams rather than living a life where you are a victim of your own nature.

- **Communicate Clearly**

Thinking through all of these things, deciding what you want to do, and even planning how you will do it's no good if you aren't voicing these ideas and communicating what you want. Use all kinds of communication at your disposal to voice your concerns and show people what you really want for yourself and what you expect from them. Empaths are fantastic listeners, and they have a knack for understanding what is going on around them, but when it comes to speaking and pushing information out, they can have trouble. Start with the circle that you are most comfortable in and start expressing yourself more freely to build this into your character and improve.

- **Take a Moment before Deciding**

People who are empaths act based on their emotions and impulse a lot more simply because they feel things so intensely. In some cases, they can't stop themselves, and it's a reflex reaction rather than a calculated decision. Whether you are saying no to a situation or agreeing to something, the important thing is not to do it in haste. Take a moment before you make a decision, step back, look at things from a different angle and then plan a course of action. This momentary pause can help you look at things from a neutral perspective, whereas in the heat of the moment, we are often driven by emotion and have a limited outlook on the matter.

The transition phase from being the person you have always been into being someone who actively implements boundaries in their life and abides by the social guidelines that they have laid is not a fast or easy transition. You should be prepared to face resistance and even be ready to lose some people. There will undoubtedly be people who will not agree with this new version of you, but that's ok. If someone is not willing to accept you for a person who stands up for themselves and has a way of doing things, they are most likely in your life for the benefit you provide them and do not want to provide you with any benefit. Over time you will grow thicker skin, making the transition phase easier to deal with. The most important thing is to stay at it in the initial phase, which is the most difficult time of the transition.

Chapter 12: How to Control Your Emotions

Managing emotions can be extremely challenging for an empath because of their natural manner of dealing with emotions, as we've discussed in previous chapters. Along with the positive, we've seen the dark side too, where an empath can go down the rabbit hole of self-destruction if they don't properly manage their emotions. They are also quite impulsive and have difficulty seeing the big picture. Even when it's an experience that doesn't have anything to do with them directly, they feel it intensely.

This impacts the way they personally feel, how they interact with other people, and how they act in their own life, and it can leave a lasting impact on their minds.

When it comes to properly managing emotions for anyone - specifically empaths - a few different stages of emotional processing can be broken down as follows: The first stage is where they are actually exposed to the stimuli, and they internalize emotions. The second stage is when they have received the message and are processing it in their minds. The last stage involves how they react to this stimulation and how they internalize the entire experience. For an empath, every stage needs to be managed. Let's look at each stage and what can be done to make the impact less potent and more manageable.

Absorbing Emotions

The first thing to address is how an empath internalizes different things going on around them. Even though it can seem relatively easy for other people to maintain a calm state when something goes wrong or are incredibly excited about something, things are very different for the empath. The empath doesn't willingly absorb things at a deep level; the problem is that they are extremely sensitive and automatically absorb things deeply and intensely, and fast. When an average person is still thinking about what they have heard, the empath is already bursting into tears, thinking of other extreme situations that will arise from this bad news. Here are a few strategies to help make the process of internalizing information a little more manageable and the impact a little less severe.

Understand the Emotion

Empaths are not only very sensitive to the emotions of others, but they are also extremely sensitive to the energy that other people bring. This is usually characterized by a situation where an empath is feeling completely normal or even slightly positive, then they either get a phone call or someone joins them, or they talk to someone, and there is a sudden and a drastic change in their emotional state. They are suddenly angry or sad, or they look like they are stressed out, and all these emotions and feelings seem to be exaggerated. As the empath, your first response to this scenario should be to work out exactly what it's you are feeling and try to identify it for yourself.

We often mix up our own feelings in the heat of the moment. When we feel excited and happy about something, we are on the brink of extreme emotion, and even something small could trigger a person to go in the opposite direction. Naming the feeling will give you more control over what is going on in your mind and give you a sense of direction. At the same time, it can help to think of the source of the emotion. Sometimes you will realize that you are angry because you just spoke to someone, telling you how frustrated they feel. Just because you feel an emotion doesn't mean that it's yours to feel. Empaths have an uncanny ability to internalize emotions that aren't theirs.

- **Ground Yourself**

There is a reason why counting sheep helps children go to sleep. This is a process known as grounding, and the aim is to get one thing that the mind can focus on so that it can stop processing the hundreds of other things going on. When you focus on one object, that object fully occupies the attention to the exclusion of anything else. It helps you let go of emotions operating in the background not related to the present moment. A great strategy is to look for something around you and focus on that or start counting from 1000 backward or mentally repeat some affirmations you remember. Anything you can do to shift your attention will help.

- **Be Self-Aware**

Check in with your feelings often and try to be as self-aware as possible, living in the present. If you have suddenly felt a change of emotion, try going back to a moment you remember just before the emotional change. When you are more self-aware, it's easier for you to bring that last good moment back and then work through what happened that brought about the change. This way, you can develop more control over how you feel even after you have gone through a major emotional change. Also, being self-aware will help you understand what it was in your surroundings that triggered the change. This way, you can better understand your triggers and why you feel these sudden changes in certain situations.

- **Visualize**

Visualization can be used in various ways to manage emotions and even manage your mind. When it comes to developing immunity against other people's emotions, it's a good idea to use some form of defensive visualization. Thinking of a thick, bulletproof glass often helps. You visualize that you are surrounded by a thick glass through which you can hear the people around you, but you cannot feel their energy. It's a kind of insulation protecting you from their energy and is giving you a small space that you can fill up with your own energy. As soon as you feel that your emotions have been changed, bring the glass into the mind, and visualize their energy on the outside and your own energy, or the emotion that you prefer at that moment, surrounding you.

- **Dig Deeper**

Sometimes we talk to someone, and we think that we understand what they mean or how they feel, whereas, in reality, they feel quite different. With your glass wall around you, take a second to ask the person to elaborate on how they feel and what is going on in their mind. This can bring you around to a perspective that you might not have previously considered, and it can help you stop feeling extreme emotion. The chances are that the person might not feel like the way they described it when they said something, or they might have meant it differently. Rather than responding based on a hunch, get down to the bottom of it and then decide how you should feel and react.

- **Reinforce Boundaries**

You have to realize that some people might just be using you for your empathic nature. They know that you will offer ears and a heart and a mind where you will feel their problem deeply. They might come to you just for this one trait alone and leave you feeling much better while making you feel horrible. This is where you need to understand your relationships and have the right kinds of boundaries in place to stop people from using you for the wrong things and stop making yourself available for the wrong things.

- **Let Go**

Sometimes, when we've spoken to the person and gotten down to the basic problem, we've highlighted our problem, but we still feel horrible. It happens; sometimes, things are just as bad as they sound, and you are right to feel the way you do. The problem is when you have absorbed the matter so deeply that you aren't willing to move on and let it go. There is a time and a place for every emotion, and once you have felt it, learned from it, and decided to move on, it's time to let that emotion go. Again, you can use visualization to help you through this process.

- **Emotional Balance**

Balancing your emotions is something that you will have to put a lot of effort into if you want to live a mentally bearable life. Many empaths don't realize that they are putting themselves through a tough time because they have grown accustomed to feeling uncomfortable. This can result in health problems, chronic mental problems, and real physical consequences of the emotional turmoil they are constantly exposed to in extreme situations.

- **Processing Your Emotions**

The first thing is to sit down with yourself and understand how you feel. Regardless of what is going on around you, what others are saying, and how you feel about others, the focus is on how you feel deep down inside. There is a chance that you are quite happy about things or that there is nothing personally troubling you, but under the burden of other people's feelings, you can't help but feel the way you do. Also, because empaths are so preoccupied with the emotions of others, they often forget to process their thoughts and feelings and never make time for themselves.

Ideally, you should be processing your feelings daily, either independently or with another person.

The process is easy and can be done in a few minutes. For instance, when you have your coffee every morning or go running in the evening, you can take that time to go through your feelings from that day. If you like to talk to someone else, discuss it with your spouse when you are in bed before going to sleep. Talk to a friend once a week when you meet up. Do anything that makes you feel comfortable, but do it regularly and do it thoroughly.

- **Putting Yourself First**

Prioritizing your feelings is really difficult for empaths as it goes against how they are designed. Even when you sit down with a spouse to talk or talk to yourself about how you feel, you can't seem to bring those emotions to the forefront. That's where you need to start focusing on your own needs and caring less about people who are not that important. The only way you can be a strong pillar for others to rely on is if you are in the right state of mind.

You can start by taking care of your body. Eating the right food, getting enough exercise, seeing the doctor regularly, all these things will help you make yourself your number one priority. Take some time for yourself daily and have some time each week to focus on doing things that you love. The positivity you'll generate will also help you better process other things in your life. Learn to celebrate your victories, not just the joys of others.

- **Moving On**

When you celebrate with a friend, it feels amazing to be in that company and feel that happiness. This is something that can bring a smile to our face even ten years later when we remember that moment. However, the negative things that we feel are also just as potent, and a bad memory can ruin your day even a decade later. The skill here is to let go of things that aren't serving you and focus on the things you truly cherish and memories that positively impact your life. This is where it really helps to have good strong boundaries that you really stick to and also have boundaries in your mind that will tell you what is yours to own and what isn't. When you start caring for yourself, celebrating the good things, and talking about your feelings regularly, it becomes easier to deal with the negative things. Otherwise, they seem to like this massive demon that you don't even want to think about, let alone tackle.

- **Managing Emotions**

The most challenging part of processing emotion as an empath is managing how these emotions manifest themselves. Being blessed with an intense ability to feel all kinds of stimuli, the way an empath expresses their feelings is unlike anyone else's. Here are a few tips to help you cope with expressing the emotional energy you feel.

- **Understand the Impact**

It's not the inherently bad emotions but rather the impact they have on our lives that's the culprit. It's good if you can feel things very intensely. It makes the experience of life that much more enjoyable and potent and makes you the unique person you are. The problem arises when you start seeing that the emotional stress you are going through impacts your relationships or negatively influences your friendship with someone. Warning bells must start ringing when it gets to a point where you feel numb to emotions, or you can feel nothing else but an overwhelming amount of that emotion.

Similarly, it's a serious problem if it's getting to the point where you can't concentrate at school or work. In many cases, people start resorting to drug abuse to somehow balance out the emotional turmoil they are going through.

All these are examples of situations where the problem is getting out of hand. This is why it's important that you realize the impact of your emotions and be careful that it doesn't impact your life.

- **Regulate Rather Than Suppress**

Some people think that simply ignoring how they feel or somehow just not addressing what is going on inside them will help to solve the issue. This is not the case; in fact, it will only backfire. When people come up with problems such as depression, suicidal thoughts, anxiety, and even physical ailments like chronic muscle pain or other diseases, there is a high possibility that this is the extra emotional pressure trying to find a way out. The mind and the body are one, and you can regulate your mind through things like meditations and therapy, and you can also regulate your body through exercise and a better diet. There is no need to feel bad about how you feel, just accept what it's and try to work through the issue.

- **Journaling**

Journaling is a very powerful tool because it not only helps you record what is happening but it gives you the time to really think about what is going on. More importantly, you must journal by hand, where you are actually writing with pen and paper rather than typing. The process of writing is also very therapeutic, and the way it impacts our brains is very different from just typing in front of a computer. Whether you journal daily or just journal when you feel like it, the ability to write helps you clarify problems in your mind and will often bring you to an idea that you had not encountered earlier when you were just brainstorming.

- **Breathing**

A lot of meditation exercises are based on breathing alone. Some people like to do chants or sing or have music playing, but simply sitting down in a quiet room in a comfortable position with your eyes closed, just focusing on your breathing, is more therapeutic than you can imagine. Not only is this an exercise in itself, but consider focusing on your breathing whenever you are going through a situation with extreme emotion. Whether you are happy or sad, just take a big deep breath, and it will recenter your thoughts. It brings more oxygen into the brain at a physical level that helps you think more clearly and drives other harmful toxins out of the brain. Take a slow deep breath, hold it for a couple of seconds, and gradually exhale. Repeat as many times as you feel necessary.

Nearly all of these management techniques will take time to master, and you will be required to be in a mindful state when you practice these exercises. In the heat of the moment, the last thing you'll remember is to give yourself space and breathe, but if you can keep this in mind and try to do it as often as you can, it will eventually become a routine and a natural response to the situation. In a way, think of this as teaching yourself how to feel again. You are re-engineering how you respond and even how your body reacts to certain stimuli.

Chapter 13: Empath Wellness

Now that we have covered the basics to let you explore your abilities, help you understand relationships, and touch on emotional management, we will be unfolding the connection between empathy and wellness in this chapter. As empaths are highly sensitive people, the surrounding energy can drastically affect emotional and physical energy. Your ability to feel the energies surrounding you and absorb them adds up to your fatigue. Furthermore, the exhaustion levels are boosted when you find it hard to escape negative energies. For other individuals, listening to music or taking a nap can be relieving, whereas an empath struggles to escape these energies, ultimately affecting wellness. Repeatedly absorbing these emotions makes you energetically exhausted. Before we go further, It's important to understand wellness. Many believe that wellness is all about improving physical well-being.

Nevertheless, that's not true at all. Think of wellness as an umbrella term, a collective of physical, mental, and spiritual well-being that keeps the body energetic, the mind relaxed, and the spirit enlightened. We'll discuss the negative effects of empathy on physical well-being, the circumstances under which an empath experiences a drain of physical energy, and ways you can practice regaining energy levels.

Empathy and Physical Well-Being

Before we explore the physical effects of negative empathy, let's be clear that we are not healthcare professionals providing advice but are only sharing this information with you after extensive research from reliable sources to help improve physical wellness. If you ever feel concerned about your health, never hesitate to contact your doctor or visit a healthcare facility near you for adequate management.

As mentioned earlier, you are greatly affected by the surrounding energies that affect your physical wellness – the combined effect of emotional and physical distress results in empath fatigue. In most cases, this burnout is not triggered suddenly. There has usually been a chain of stressful events or experiences leading up to this empath fatigue. Mental, physical, and spiritual well-being are all affected, and repeated exposure to traumatic events can lead to a person experiencing emotional and physical effects.

Physical Effects

- Sudden and frequent headaches occur anytime throughout the day or night.
- Being unproductive while performing everyday tasks.

- Infrequent sleep and increased symptoms of sleeplessness.

- Experiencing the feeling of nausea and vomiting most of the time. This feeling of fullness decreases your food intake drastically, leading to malnutrition.

- Feeling exhausted, having low energy levels, and an unwillingness to perform daily activities.

- Triggers poor changes in the appetite.

- Can lead to drug abuse or self-medication in search of finding a remedy for the physical effects.

- Avoiding activities related to the workplace and not getting involved in interacting with people due to low physical energy.

Emotional Effects

Empath fatigue is an accumulation of emotional and physical effects. Let's read about the emotional effects mentioned below.

- Limiting your social circle and not being willing to meet anyone.

- Experiencing an elevated sense of numbness.

- Feeling a lack of energy and avoiding interaction with people.

- Not being able to connect with others.

- Feeling angry, depressed, hopeless, and powerless while doing the simplest of tasks.

- Increased thoughts about the suffering that other people go through.

- Losing the sense of time and space at times.

- Blaming oneself for the problems.

The physical and emotional effects pile up day after day, resulting in empathy fatigue. This constant stress due to traumatic events and feeling the pain of others further aggravates depression and anxiety, and that decreases physical wellness. Let's quickly review your body's physical response to anxiety and depression.

The Body's Response to Anxiety and Depression

Anxiety and depression occur due to constant emotional triggers that ultimately lead to physical responses. As empathy fatigue adds up to depression and anxiety, you could experience physical effects like stomach pain, lightheadedness, and even result in cardiovascular diseases. Obesity and chronic pain are some other manifestations that can occur due to depression and anxiety. Furthermore, serotonin levels decrease significantly, resulting in poor sleep, digestion, and metabolism. Serotonin is a key hormone produced by the brain that stabilizes the mood, makes us feel happy content, and aids in improving communication functions of the brain.

Working out an exercise routine can also be beneficial in improving your physical wellness and helping lower anxiety and depression levels that build up in an empath. Studies suggest that following a physical exercise routine is as effective as taking antidepressant medications. Besides improving the blood flow to vital organs, promoting growth, and boosting the immune system, exercise releases endorphins in your body that can revitalize your body, elevate your mood, and start experiencing events in a positive light over time.

Furthermore, exercise helps stretch the muscles that relieve tension in the body, making you feel relaxed. As the mind and body are closely linked, improved physical wellness gives you the power to ward off negative energies, save your physical energy from getting depleted, and help you revitalize within no time.

Not only that, but exercise is also a great lifestyle modification you can focus on to help you get over the trauma or the negative energies affecting your well-being. Adding up the benefits of exercise, you should have improved memory, higher self-esteem, and resilience when faced with mental and emotional challenges. Before you start an exercise routine, it's best to consult the related healthcare professionals and get yourself evaluated or get recommendations for the safest exercises for you to do.

Diet and Empathy

As mentioned previously, empathy is a powerful gift that can reap tons of benefits when you can completely practice self-care. Focusing on what you eat in your diet is a crucial aspect of self-care that we empaths have to learn to get the best possible outcome in terms of wellness. As empaths, negative emotions and mood swings can disrupt digestion, leading to symptoms like bloating and abdominal discomfort. When an empathetic person is already overwhelmed with emotions, many foods can further disrupt the digestive system.

Instead of listening to others for diet recommendations, trusting your body is the best way to know the foods that keep your digestive system healthy and make you feel comfortable. Here are some diet recommendations you can try to support your physical wellness better.

- Staying conscious of your body's response to consumption of certain foods and noting information to create a diet that works for you.

- Go for warm water instead of cold water and replace beverages with herbal teas.

- Eat foods that are cooked well can help digest. However, it does not mean that you should skip eating raw fruits and vegetables. Try understanding your body's response and select the adequate foods for the best results.

- Avoid excess chilies and use spices like cinnamon, ginger, or turmeric to help improve digestion.
- Make a schedule of meal times and stick to it, which will maintain consistent bowel movements.
- Chewing your food and eating slowly also helps greatly with digestion.

Most people follow diet plans to control certain diseases. For example, people with inflammatory bowel syndrome avoid eating dairy products as it can aggravate the disease. Similarly, food influences the traits of empaths. For example, most processed foods contain chemicals that make you crave these foods, ultimately making the urge unbearable. Consuming these poorly nutritious foods affects the body physically and leads to endocrine and hormonal changes that further deteriorate physical wellness.

Undoubtedly, negative emotions take a toll on physical wellness, but the chemicals found in our food can also negatively affect the body, making you feel low on energy. By following an appropriate self-care routine and focusing on improving diet, you can improve energy levels. Besides feeling energized, your ability to perform tasks increases, and your goals become clearer.

Why Empaths Feel Drained

Whatever type of energy is in the immediate environment, empaths quickly assimilate and register it and get affected without understanding the consequences or how it even happened. The suffering and emotions surrounding you will trigger responses to help others while not knowing how to protect your energy. Let's explore the causes that drain up your energy, leaving you with a feeling of physical exhaustion.

- **Hyper-Perceptive to Emotions**

We all have friends that never get tired or feel drained, but for an empath, you need to take care of your personal space to conserve energy because of the consequences you will suffer. Interacting with a lot of energies at once results in physical exhaustion that can further manifest symptoms that affect your body. It takes a lot more time to reset energy levels when you are overwhelmed by the emotions and energies you encounter throughout the day.

- **A Sensitive Body**

Most empaths feel emotional sensitivity up to a level that starts negatively interacting with their physical bodies. Each empath is unique and responds differently to physical stimuli. The threshold of physical stimuli for empaths varies and changes over time. However, life and circumstances can help empaths deal with the physical pressure and develop tolerance. For example, if you are working at a hospital, you might feel an emotional and physical overload at first, but after a few weeks, you will naturally develop resistance towards these emotions as you start managing your sensitivity levels. You are naturally wired to feel the energies around you and perceive the emotions of others like your own. Using this ability to profoundly connect with others instead of becoming overstimulated by the energy is a technique that empaths need to practice maintaining their energy levels.

- **Physical Spaces**

You are picky about the physical spaces you interact with. Most empaths prefer a soft and ambient environment that helps them recharge and enjoy their time. Visiting physical places that emit negative vibes constantly drains your energy levels, leaving you physically overburdened and exhausted. We all have a finite amount of energy that fuels our body to perform everyday tasks.

- **Experiencing Collective Energy**

Planetary shifts like changes in weather, temperature, earthquakes, and related geological changes influence the energy levels of empaths. Conserving your energy by practicing grounding routines will do you a lot of good.

- **Poor Self-Awareness**

Caregivers put the needs of others ahead of their own and bother less about themselves. This constant caregiving routine for an empath can quickly deplete energy levels, making it hard to continue the same routine. Neglecting your needs like not resting enough, eating a bad diet, and overexercising will all take a toll on physical wellness.

Only a tender heart can feel someone else's pain and suffering. There are times when empaths start absorbing too much like an energy sponge that greatly affects their physical well-being. This overload of emotional and physical stress makes you less compassionate. The key to being compassionate to others is to practice self-compassion first. By doing this, you reserve energy and stamina to be compassionate and help heal your own empathy fatigue.

- **Protecting Your Energy**

As we've said in previous chapters, being an empath can be likened to having a superpower that gives you the ability to interpret and feel various forms of energy around you. This beautiful gift of feeling others' energies can become a nuisance if you don't know how to manage your energy reserves to avoid getting physically drained. Here are some tips and lifestyle modifications you can practice in your daily life to be in control of your energy.

- **Setting up Boundaries**

One of the most important things for an empath to do is to set up clear boundaries in relationships, social life, and at work. It might be one of the hardest things to do for you, but setting up boundaries that define your physical space is crucial. Explore your boundaries, set rules, and try not to let your guard down. Remember that these interventions protect your energy and wellness, not deny others the help or genuine emotional support that they might require from you. Empaths might consider setting up boundaries with being selfish for oneself. However, that's not the case, as these boundaries will define you as a person with clear priorities. Staying honest about your willingness to help others and saying being clear on what you want or not can help you better take care of your energy.

- **Daily Meditation**

Besides incorporating an exercise routine and changing your dietary habits, practicing a daily meditation routine will most likely relax your mind, boost up your energy, and improve your physical well-being.

- **Be Aware**

Figuring out the type of interactions and people who deplete your energy is a great way to understand how you feel. After an interaction, you might feel either energized and uplifted or drained of all your energy. As a highly sensitive person, it's essential to be selective of the company you spend time with and recognize the interactions that make you feel good or drained. In addition to recognizing your comfort levels, note down what choices you are making, because as empaths, the energies you absorb from your surroundings have a physiological impact on your well-being. Getting familiar with your baseline energy levels and differentiating your emotions from others can help you manage your physical energy and stop it from depleting.

Throughout the day, take note of the moments that help you get energized and practice avoiding the moments that ultimately put you in a chronic state of exhaustion. As you start improving your energy levels, appreciate your progress, no matter how small, to keep you motivated to achieve better results. Cherishing these moments uplifts your spirits, makes you feel revitalized and leads you to a direction that eases out fatigue.

- **Acting Responsibly**

You always take on or try to share the trauma and suffering of others that only drains your physical energy without resulting in any fruitful outcomes. Taking responsibility for the energy you are emitting and knowing that you are not responsible for someone else's emotions or that you don't have to lend a helping hand every time they ask for it.

- **Spend Time Alone**

A drain of physical energy renders you unable to carry out daily activities effectively. Giving your body time to relax, recharge, and replenish the energy is essential. With as little interaction with people as possible, spend your time in nature. Relax at home, or book a vacation but be sure that you spend enough time in nature to absorb the positive energy.

- **Maintaining Balance**

Striking a balance between things is an essential aspect that should be worked upon. For example, balancing your work and personal life is a crucial aspect that almost every individual tries to improve. Likewise, maintaining a balance between the self-care routine and the pain and suffering you feel for others is an essential task to do. When you're feeling stressed out, relax and work on ways you can balance your everyday routine and get the best possible results.

- **Asking for Help**

Whether it's family, friends, relationships, or support groups, never hesitate to reach out for help if you are in a constant caregiving position and share the responsibilities to get that much-needed rest.

- **Adequate Sleep**

Following an adequate sleep routine is essential for an empath to revitalize and restore their depleted energy levels. Overstimulation of senses throughout the day is naturally calmed during deep sleep of the sleep cycle. Our sleep is divided into different stages, out of which deep sleep or slow-wave sleep is the third one. Sleep hygiene is essential to follow a better sleep routine. You find the refuge of your bed satisfying when it's comfortable, placed somewhere quiet, and is surrounded by a peaceful environment.

The feeling of being physically and emotionally overwhelmed makes it hard to sleep adequately. You can consider practicing meditation or practice yoga to help regulate your sleep cycle. Listening to natural sounds of rainfall, water, and nature can help rejuvenate your senses while you drift away into a deep sleep. Some people also get so stuck in a traumatic life event that it affects their daily sleep patterns.

- **Establishing Connections**

Human connections are an important aspect that can easily affect when experiencing an energy drain. Establishing new connections with people becomes difficult as you don't feel like you have adequate physical and emotional energy. Understanding why you need to connect and rediscovering your purpose can fuel up your energy levels.

- **Spending Time**

Laughter and enjoyment are two emotions to cherish with friends and your loved ones. During a burnout, it might be hard to plan on your own. You can consider spending time with friends and family who genuinely feel your burden and who will help you out through stressful times.

Empaths are energetic beings who can feel the surrounding energy affecting their emotions, physical energy, and well-being. Each interaction with the outside world is an energy exchange that empaths can feel within themselves. This unprecedented ability to feel gives empaths the ultimate power to heal others and connect with them emotionally. However, being unwilling to look into yourself and neglecting self-care is what takes a toll on physical energy and wellness.

Chapter 14: Mastering Your Mental Energy

Humans are naturally hardwired to feel other people's pain and empathize with them. This empathy influences us to help, volunteer, and even go for careers related to the service industry. We are more than connected in this technological age, especially through digital and social media platforms. However, this increased connectivity leaves a debilitating impact on the emotions of an empath. When highly sensitive people like empaths practice altruism and empathy without incorporating self-care in their lives, it leads to an emotionally compromised state followed by depression and anxiety. Controlling your emotional responses during these times is necessary because the build-up of negative energies will ultimately drain your mental energy if it goes too far. This chapter will discuss how your mental energy gets affected and share with you steps to help you regain focus and clarity of mind.

Virtually every metabolic process occurring within our body requires energy. Similarly, when being empathetic, energy is used that can deplete your mental resources. Many jobs and workplaces like prisons, hospitals, day-care facilities leave a person in these emotionally charged industries open to becoming seriously exhausted if they are not mindful of keeping their mental resources protected. Every person has a threshold for how much empathy they can offer. After that, the emotional overload starts taking a mental, physical, and spiritual toll.

Situations That Affect Mental Energy

Several situations can be mentally exhausting for an empath and result in an energy drain, leaving the mind clouded, decreasing the ability to concentrate, and slowing down cognitive functioning. Below are some situations empaths find mentally challenging.

- Trying to be recognized among peers and get accepted
- When guilt rises due to repeated self-blame after experiencing negative energy
- Forcing yourself to act upon everything and perceive responding as an obligation

- When interacting with people who are not true to you or are holding back and not opening up to you
- After experiencing a situation where you have been taken advantage of
- Constant emotional fatigue leads to mental distress
- Violence or horror deeply upsets you.
- Carrying on with relationships that lack a true and sincere bonding
- Interacting with people or meeting up with overly dramatic people
- Facing abuse from peers
- When feeling insecure, unwelcome, or don't feel like you are at the right place

Besides the situations mentioned above, evaluate your routine when at work, around people, and at home to recognize the situations' effect on you. Furthermore, pay attention to each situation you encounter and ask whether facing these situations would be fruitful or not.

Utilizing Your Mental Energy

Here are some steps you can incorporate into your daily life to gain control of your mental energy and redirect it into a skill that improves your mental well-being rather than depletes it. You might be compelled to take every responsibility that comes up, but it will only make you unable to manage your mental energy.

- **Set Boundaries**

As mentioned in the previous chapter, it's essential to recognize yourself, your priorities, goals, and the path you want to carry on in your life. After getting a complete understanding of what you want, set up boundaries according to your preferences. As you are softhearted, most people might just want your company or take advantage of your caring nature. Therefore, it's up to you to decide what to take on and the things you need to let go of, as only you can be the one responsible for your own physical and mental well-being. Setting up boundaries does not mean that you have to stop being a caring person. The point is that you only have to help when it's required and after ensuring that there will be no negative effects that could disturb your mental energy.

- **Develop a Strong Personality**

Developing a strong and well-defined personality at social gatherings or work is essential. Empathizing with people and experiencing emotions on different levels slightly changes the identity of empaths. This fluctuation in the personality can drastically affect your relationships as the personality changes can result in mistrust. This mistrust triggers an emotional surge that affects physical and mental wellness. Instead of modifying your habits and faking emotions to please others, act naturally and let them recognize your true self. Allowing others to tell you how to act is never an option as it can lead to you being manipulated and abused.

- **Building up Self-Confidence**

Mentally draining situations are not a problem when you have enough self-confidence. When working in teams, empaths feel guilty about not being accepted and can develop insecurities if they are faced with people emitting negative vibes. It's easy to recognize what others are thinking about you as an empath. Boosting your self-esteem is essential if you are encountering such an issue. Tell yourself that no one in this world is perfect and try to accept the situation as it's without feeling bad or becoming overwhelmed by thinking about others' opinions of you.

- **Company Matters**

The people surrounding you define the levels of mental energy you will be carrying through the day. By following an objective approach, refine your social circle and surround yourself with people that support you. If someone is being abusive, ignore them. You might lose a lot of friends in the process, but the ones left will be those who truly cherish and enjoy your company.

- **Handling Distress**

Being compassionate is a form of emotional empathy that we all practice at different levels. Taking on others' problems and making them our own might win us great appreciation in society, but the risks to our mental heal can be disastrous. Instead, redirect your mental energy into practicing compassion, a mild form of empathy that provides a way to use your mental energy and empathy in adequate proportions. Whenever you are experiencing mental or physical pain after being exposed to trauma or suffering, remind yourself that the situation you are experiencing is not happening to you.

- **Filter Your Consumption**

Your body and mind react to what you take in, especially in the form of news. Take social media as an example. When working at your office, imagine taking a quick peek at your news feed, and you are bombarded with information and news that triggers a shift of energy that clouds the mind, slows down cognitive abilities, and lowers your mental energy. If you feel stressed out after a few minutes of social media usage, try giving it a break for a day or two. Don't worry that you'll miss out on anything important as you will always hear about a major event or news from friends and family around you. The point of limiting social media usage is to prevent exposure to events and the type of news that only makes you emotionally drained. By avoiding the things that make you upset, you will gradually control your emotional and cognitive abilities.

- **Maintain an Objective Approach**

Just like emotional management, try to figure out the feelings that make you energetic and the ones that drain you. Be in control and avoid getting exposed to emotional situations. After all, it's your thoughts and your decision to give priority to them. As empaths, you are always open to energy and feel almost every type of energy at a certain level. How the energy affects you depends on the intensity with which you perceive it. If you try to see a certain situation from a different perspective, its effect on your mental energy decreases. Furthermore, controlling your work environment is essential if you want a clear and productive mind. Working in workplaces with open floors and maximum interaction might not be conducive for an empath. Remote working is a better choice for empaths as it will help conserve our energy without depleting it.

- **Practice Clarity**

Whenever we see ourselves get ignored by our peers or the ideas we pitch in at the office get turned down, negativity starts to develop, weakening our cognitive abilities and lowering mental energy. If left unresolved, the negativity gets contagious and affects your mood, productivity, and work efficiency. As empaths are energy beings, visualizing a protective aura around you can help prevent you from picking up negative feelings that use up your mental energy.

- **Relax Your Mind**

Negative emotions affect you one way or another. When interacting in the office or socializing with peers, they can take hold of your mind, use up all your mental energy, and result in physical manifestations like increased muscle tension and an elevated heart rate. Calming your nerves can help lower the emotions triggered after encountering negative energies. During a stressful event like experiencing the pain of others, meditation or breathing exercises can significantly help release mental stress build-up. Be in control of your thoughts and stop pondering over any form of negative energy. Instead, shift your focus to relaxing thoughts. Shifting your thought process and aggravating constructive thoughts will help you attain peace of mind and clear foresight.

- **Setting up Priorities**

As an empath, you have to cope with things that come up every day. You might be able to resolve a few issues bothering you, but many issues in one day will drain you. Trying to control everything around you might not be possible, and you'll end up frustrated. The less you focus on irrelevant things, the more energy you have to tackle the important things. Therefore, prioritize what you want to focus on and avoid wasting your energy on useless experiences.

- **Managing Negative Energy**

There is a plethora of emotions like anger, disgust, fear, grief, insecurity, and internal conflict that interfere with your ability to analyze the situation you are putting yourself into, cloud your judgment, and deprive you of mental energy. Besides focusing on positive emotions and avoiding thinking about negative ones, you can try several different techniques like exercise, meditation, ignoring the cause of negative emotions, and reviewing emotions in a positive light to ward off the negative effects of emotions on your mental health well-being.

- **Detox**

Empaths can sense the energy with which they are interacting. Even the type of food we consume has vibrational energy to mitigate mental stress. Eating vegetables, fruits, herbal teas, and whole foods will help to strengthen your mind, whereas low vibrational foods like poultry and milk products can negatively affect mental well-being. In addition, exercise helps clear out any bad energy, helps in detoxification, and triggers the production of happy hormones, making your mind sharp and clear.

- **Self-Care**

Besides working on your mental energy, implementing a self-care routine is also an essential aspect to consider. Here are some quick tips on the type of self-care routines you can follow to help calm down your overstimulated nerves for better energy control.

1. Adding bath salts and essential oils to your bath will add up to the calming effect.

2. There are a lot of massage techniques used to regain mental focus - as a relaxed body will help the mind to work effectively.

3. Spending time with animals can help change your mood from negative to positive.

4. Choose activities like Reiki, music, and meditations.

5. Listening to positive affirmations can help you ward off negative energy build-up when you're mentally stressed out.

6. When feeling mentally exhausted, try doing activities that make you laugh. Watching your favorite comedian crack jokes is a good way to help soothe those overexcited nerve endings.

7. Using essential oils can also create an ambient environment around you, making it easy to relieve anxiety stress and strengthen your brain over time.

8. Meditation and journaling can help you recognize your thoughts and feelings if you find it hard to be clear.

Recognizing Empathy Skills

There are several downsides of being an empath, and some empath attributes can be turned into skills to boost productivity and efficiency. Practicing empathy while being extremely aware of your inner self creates a sense of happiness and wholeness. Your unique abilities and skills can even be used in several professions for the benefit of many. Let's read about the empathy gifts you possess that can be used as a skill at work, home, or when socializing.

- **Self-Awareness**

Empaths devote themselves to developing an understanding of their feelings and connecting to the energies around them. Use your experience to learn to improve your self-awareness by knowing your limits and the number of interactions you can easily handle. An empath with a strongly developed sense of self-awareness not only makes you happy but also helps others by letting you deliver effectively. To explore more on self-awareness, you need to be connected more to yourself. Asking yourself the questions will help develop better self-awareness that leads to better growth and allow you to regulate your mental energy as required.

- **Observation and Perception**

Being highly perceptive, having great observation skills, and registering the types of energies you interact with our natural skills that only empaths possess. As empaths can easily recognize surrounding energies, this gift can effectively empathize with people. Recognizing this ability to have a deeper perception of things can be used to help differentiate genuine feelings from fake ones. Using your energy recognition capabilities, the underlying issues of the other person can be understood and be guided to move forward with life.

- **A Simple Life**

Being an empath requires you to reset, revitalize, and ground your energies from time to time. Experiencing a surge of energy and emotions can make an empath exhausted. That's the reason most empaths are drawn to live in quiet, peaceful places where they can tune in with the surrounding energy vibrations.

- **Being Creative**

Due to their highly sensitive nature, empaths can express themselves extensively through their creative abilities. The way they communicate and connect deeply with the surrounding environment gives them the skill to express themselves fluently through impactful words or help others find energetic balance.

- **Healing Others**

Empaths can regulate energy and heal others. This gift to sense other people's plight and the trauma without exchanging words is what makes empaths unique. This skill can be used for the benefit of society. Empaths who recognize this opt for careers where they can put it to good use – like working in healthcare facilities and hospitals. As you learn to use your special healing skills, you will naturally be able to tell if your help is not required. The gifts of an empath allow them to see the possible paths of healing or help needed. However, it's up to the person seeking help to take your advice or leave it.

- **Quality of Life**

As you start looking at your traits as gifts and start mastering control over your mental energy, you will be able to get aligned with the energies of this world, explore your true self, and live life the way you want it to. Using these skills to your advantage helps improve the quality of life.

- **Socializing Skills**

When empaths keep mental distress to a minimum, they can suffer serious negative effects, especially when socializing. By understanding how you are affected by someone else's energy, you can decide on the best way to approach them. This skill can be used at the workplace, while communicating, and even in relationships.

It's pretty easy for an empath to get caught up in life as you will be experiencing different forms of seen or unseen energies along the way. However, effectively recognizing your abilities and using them adequately can help you stay healthy and let you have control over your physical and mental energy. Remember that you are here to enjoy life to its fullest. With time, you will experience joy, happiness, sadness, failure, success, triumph, and every other related physical or emotional trigger. Therefore, never hesitate and enjoy life in all its variety. As you explore your journey as an empath, it's best to join support groups or find like-minded people through digital platforms, as it will help create a support network to provide you with the relevant assistance and the ability to navigate this world. Recognizing what others feel is an asset that a few possess. With these abilities, it's easier for you to screen out genuine people from fake ones in any situation.

Chapter 15: Empath in a Cruel World

Imagine you're walking around the mall, just looking around the shops and taking a closer look at whatever catches your eye. You hear a couple arguing, a baby crying, and a frustrated mother, all a couple of steps away. These are everyday occurrences, right? These are all things that are bound to happen wherever there are people. But being an empath, you try to get away as quickly as possible. It's already too late, though. You feel a weird sensation in your stomach as anger and frustration start boiling up inside of you for no apparent reason. Only you know why you're absorbing what's going on around you, and you already know your day is going to be difficult to navigate.

When you touch something or someone you believe is weak, you feel an unsettling sensation. You may lean on a tree or touch an animal, and you can just tell that they're sad. You feel this odd sensation that only disappears when you take your hands off the subject. By now, you have realized that these are not your own emotions, but they feel like they are. Passing by a group of angry people, like rallies, can make you feel sick to your stomach. You feel the tension in the room when no one else notices, and you can almost tell what a person is like before you get to know them. You also just know if someone is a good person or if something doesn't sit right with them. Your first impressions are spot on.

It's even worse if you find yourself surrounded by a group of unhealthy individuals; it literally tears you down. Exposing yourself to several peoples' energies at once can be emotionally and physically draining. Even if your friends aren't necessarily unhealthy, everyone has their battles to fight and be an empath. This is why you can feel everything- the pain, the anger, the sadness, the cries for help, and the desperation. People say that they're fine even when they're wounded inside, which is why you can't just ask how someone is doing and move on with your life. Everyone lies about their feelings. We all know that everyone does it, but non-empaths don't think much of it. However, being an empath makes you wonder how and why we have all been trained to deny and lie about our feelings.

While it's undeniably difficult to live life knowing all about other people's predicaments, this ability is quite enriching. You get to be involved in the human experience more than any other human, which other people don't think is possible. Your encounters are always intricate and dynamic.

These things happen to you all the time. You can't just get rid of these experiences, or turn them off, no matter how hard you try. You explain to your friends repeatedly that you can't do anything about it, but they just don't understand. Being an empath makes you the peacemaker of all your social groups. It's a given since you feel upset whenever anyone else feels sad, which is why you always try to resolve conflicts before they even begin.

Being an empath in the world we live in today is a challenge. Sometimes it feels like the world is becoming more and more violent. Perhaps it's because technology and social media have made it possible for us to learn about gruesome global happenings in an instant. Maybe people are just becoming crueler by the day.

The chances are that the pandemic has also made it harder for you. The soaring number of deaths, people in pain, and the rise in mental illness rates are enough to make you suffer.

If you think about it, being an empath is like being naturally academically gifted. During the first few stages of elementary school, you believe that everyone is like you. However, as you grow and make it to middle school then high school, you realize that you're gifted in a sense, which puts you at an advantage. You learned t you can understand, in a deeper sense, how and why you stand out. In your case, you understand that you can find out why you tap into what you sense in other people's emotions. Once you become masterful enough, you can even help others develop these abilities, regardless of whether they were naturally gifted with it. Most people can develop and enhance their empathetic abilities unless they have certain personality disorders that get in the way.

You may have always despised your abilities as an empath. However, if you think about it, would you really want to trade your brain for a normally functioning one? Sure, it gets tiring at times, but learning how to gain control of your reactions and separate your feelings from those around you will allow you to realize that you possess a wonderful gift.

This chapter will help you understand your fears about living in today's society, as well as how you can address them. You will find out how you can find your internal safe and peaceful place and manage the emotions elicited by the events that happen around you. You'll also find out how to keep societal issues and anxieties at bay.

Addressing Societal Fears

Being an empath comes with numerous societal and emotional triggers. Certain events or situations can trigger an overload, making you feel emotionally exhausted, anxious, and even depressed. The word "triggered" is something that we keep hearing more and more nowadays. People are throwing the word around carelessly, often in the incorrect context. So, what does it really mean to be triggered? A triggered individual is deeply impacted by overwhelming emotions that result from a traumatic event, situation, or memory. The minds of empaths tend to develop specific triggers after witnessing overly sensitive events. If severe enough, the individual could develop PTSD.

In most cases, an empath's mind will come up with a very chaotic loop of unending feelings, which would cause great distress. Empaths get triggered by the slightest incidents. They have no control over their undesirable emotions and sensory overload. This is why empaths are likely to develop fears that affect their ability to navigate the outside world.

We collected some emotional triggers that you may encounter in your society and how you can address them in a healthy way.

Feeling Misunderstood

Many people don't bother to take the time to understand others. If you're an empath, this is something that you may struggle to wrap your head around because you are naturally going to be able to understand people and be empathetic with them. So, you can't help but fear the apathy of those around you. The chances are that you've been used, made fun of, or called "dramatic," "weird," or other ignorant terms, at least a couple of times during your lifetime. This may be why you're probably very afraid of being misunderstood. Being understood is something you long for, which often leaves you doubting yourself. You start to wonder if you're really odd, unintelligent, or even crazy. You may wonder if something is wrong with you because no one seems to understand how your brain is wired.

If you want to address this issue, then the first thing to know is that there is nothing wrong with you. Your empathy doesn't make you odd, crazy, or unintelligent. Your gift makes you *very* emotionally intelligent. Your ability to dig deep into other people's feelings and emotions is incredible. You should remind yourself that no one needs to learn about how you think or how your brain works. As long as you're always working on understanding it and putting your abilities to their best use, then you're good to go. Find comfort, or rather power, in being misunderstood. Your abilities make you unique. Your ability to think in a way that's so foreign to others puts you at an advantage. So, the next time someone tries to make you feel inadequate, remember that they probably feel threatened by your extraordinary sensations and perceptions.

Feeling Unwanted

Our world is very cruel. People like to hurt and tear down what they don't understand, and as we explained above, many people don't understand you. They don't understand your ability to tap into the energies of others or your heightened intuitive senses. The fact that you can tell exactly how they're feeling can frighten them. Fear is at the bottom of so many things that make you unhappy because people simply don't understand you, and with that misunderstanding comes alienation. All the while, you are picking up on these emotions and trying to make sense of them. You may feel like an imposter and wonder why anyone would actually want you around. It helps to remind yourself that these are just intrusive thoughts. Having been abandoned once or encountering people who intentionally make you feel inadequate doesn't mean that intentionally making you feel inadequate doesn't mean you're not wanted. You are more than your empathy. While there are people out there that will love you for it, they will also love you for all the other traits that make you who you are. If someone doesn't love or want you wholly, know that they're toxic and that it would be time to reconsider your relationship or friendship with them.

Feeling Valueless

If you're an empath, you probably have difficulty saying no, even when saying yes compromises your general well-being. Aside from the compelling need to help those around you, part of the reason why you rush to cater to the needs of others may be because you want to feel valued. You probably already know that some people may use you for your kindness and compassion, which feeds into your fear of being worthless. As counterintuitive as it sounds, you become more and more obsessed with ensuring that all the needs of others are fulfilled. Reinforcing the idea that you may be perceived as "less than" can cause you to lose yourself in a spiral of unwanted harmful emotions. Once you find yourself stuck in that hole, it can feel impossible to make your way out.

If you're struggling with feelings of being unworthy, always remember that everyone on Earth has a certain purpose or value, particularly you. You were blessed with these unique abilities for a reason. If anything, they increase your value and not diminish it. You should take the time to think about what self-worth means to you. Do you think someone else would be unworthy just because they care a little bit more about others? Aim to destroy these false perceptions about yourself because your power to feel the emotions of others is extremely valuable. The world needs more people like you. Indulge in activities that can help boost your self-esteem and raise your vibrations. Take the time to practice self-care and recite positive affirmations.

Feeling Unloved

As an empath, you are characterized by your excessive compassion and tendency to nourish others. Other people may not express their feelings the same way that you do, making you feel unloved. Because you have so much love to give, there is a great fear inside you – you think your feelings are never reciprocated. This is why many empaths end up isolated in an effort to protect themselves from potential heartbreak. You may even have thought about shutting everyone in your life out to save yourself the hurt. The need to feel loved is natural. However, running away from social life is not a solution because the fact is that you've always been loved. From the moment you were born, there were always people who loved you and cared about you. This is why you shouldn't let the lack of reciprocation break you in any way.

Not Feeling Accepted

While growing up, there have been many times when you felt left out. There may have been things or activities that you've had to sit out because your empathy got in the way. These moments may have made you question whether you are actually accepted in your community. We tend to attach our self-worth to how much we're loved and accepted by others. This can be very damaging because everyone is worthy, regardless of how others perceive them. You can't be loved, accepted, and understood by everyone, even if these are things that you give to the world. You're an empath, but not everyone else is. So, it only makes sense that you focus on the relationships and friendships that already make you feel loved, valued, and potentially understood.

The Inability to Just "Get Over It"

How many times have you been told to just "get over it?" You've probably tried time and time again, believing that your reactions were over the top. Questions like "is there something wrong with me?" and "why am I too sensitive?" may have clouded your brain. You may have always feared the possibility of never being able to just get over it. However, remember people don't spend as much time thinking about the words that come out of their mouths as you do. You strongly feel for others and everything that you experience, so just getting over it, at least overnight, is not possible. In fact, you don't even need to get over your experiences. All you need to do is move forward and grow around them.

News and Society

As mentioned above, technological breakthroughs and social media have made learning about different events and news worldwide. Unfortunately, the world is not a nice place, which is why you may constantly inevitably hear about things that make you sick to the stomach. Some news may even make you horrified about leaving your home or interacting with others altogether. However, you should be avoiding the news and not people instead. To thrive as an empath, you need to be part of your society and not a product of it, which is why you should contribute positively through charity, volunteer work, environmental clean-ups, and more.

Self-Protection Methods

Practicing self-protection strategies and incorporating them into your life and routine can help you navigate life as well. These exercises can be extremely helpful whenever you're feeling stressed or absorbing too much of the negativity of others. There are numerous strategies to help you release your stress, worries, and unwanted emotions – experiment to find the ones that work best for you.

Symptom Separation

Whenever you're feeling upset or experiencing a sensory overload, take time to think about whether these emotions belong to you or to someone else. If there's no apparent reason behind the way you're feeling or experiencing a sudden change in a physical sensation or mood, then you're probably absorbing the symptoms of someone else. In this case, try to indulge in activities that calm you, such as practicing grounding techniques, deep breathing, or walking around in nature.

Get Away

Once you identify what's bothering or unsettling you, you need to get away from whatever is disturbing you. See if you're calmer and more relieved. You may worry about offending others. However, you need to start putting your well-being first. If you're in a park, a movie theater, or even a doctor's office, change seats to get away from the source. If you feel uncomfortable in a certain restaurant or cafe, always remember that you don't have to stay there. You can find your peace and enjoy being somewhere else. It's fine to say no and seek refuge from overwhelming locations and situations. You need time to recharge and recollect yourself.

Set Boundaries

If you're an empath, then you already know that nothing transfers energy faster than physical touch, and of course, the eyes. If someone makes you feel uncomfortable, limit physical touch and eye contact. Always remember that hugs and other physical interactions are a choice and that no one is entitled to overstep your boundaries.

Aside from physical interactions, you need to set general limits with people, especially those who drain your energy. You are in control of the time you spend listening to others and giving them advice. You don't need to be at the beck and call of others, go to all outings, or cater to their requests. It will take a lot of time to change how you communicate and interact with others. However, a change like this is necessary to ensure your physical, mental, and emotional well-being.

Practice Earthing

Empaths have a built-in inclination to spend time in nature. They love it and find peace there. Surrounding yourself with a green and clean environment can help rid you of negative energy and feelings. The Earth promotes inner healing. You can walk barefoot in the sand, grass, or soil and pay attention to how it feels. You can also lie down in the meadows or meditate outdoors.

Go Offline

Take regular breaks from social media and technology. These devices give us way too much information, which is the last thing that you need as an empath. Avoid using your phone for at least half an hour first thing in the morning and before you go to bed. The things you see online can set the tone for the rest of the day and hinder the quality of your sleep. You should also avoid going online often throughout the day. Make sure that you take sufficient breaks during the day and avoid visiting resources you know may trigger you.

If you're an empath, you are probably overwhelmed with social anxiety. You are always extremely conscious of people's emotions and, therefore, always hyper-aware of everything that comes out of your mouth. You've trained yourself to choose your words carefully, which is why it can always feel like you're walking on eggshells whenever you're in a group. You may have developed various fears throughout your upbringing due to your abilities. Fortunately, there are numerous ways to address them and navigate life in a healthier way.

Chapter 16: Embracing Your Spirit

In the last chapter of this book, we will focus on an empath's spiritual life. A highly sensitive person might feel out of place in a world that's not designed for them, but when they connect to their spirit and essence, they know they are one with "all." The purpose of this chapter is to equip you with methods on how to achieve this connection - particularly through meditation. You can also find some tips on setting up a daily spiritual routine and what you can do in this routine.

What Is Spirituality and Why Is It Important?

Spirituality is the experience of connecting with something greater than ourselves. It might be a sense of oneness with the universe or a feeling of deep peace and love. For an empath, it can be essential to connect with their Spirit to feel grounded and aligned.

When we connect with our spirit, we become more authentic and self-aware. Our spirit represents truth and authenticity, while we represent creativity and uniqueness. When these two meet, they bring forth the best of us - our essence or heart space.

Spirituality Could Mean Different Things for Different People

Spirituality doesn't have to mean anything specific. It could be praying, meditating, being in nature, or even just taking some time for yourself each day. The important thing is that it connects you with your innermost desires and brings forth a sense of peace and joy.

For example, some people like to meditate, while others enjoy yoga or walking in the park. As long as you are doing it for your own good and not anyone else's, then all is well!

Identifying What Works for You

The key to embracing your spirit's finding what works for you. There is no right or wrong way to do this, as long as it brings you closer to who you truly are. The best way to find out is to experiment and see what feels good. Some ideas to try are:

Meditating can be done by anyone regardless of your spiritual beliefs. This helps you quieten the mind and connect with "all." If this stresses out an empath or highly sensitive person, don't force it. Try walking in nature instead, with natural serenity to help ground you.

Writing in your journal or creating art is fun and insightful because both allow us to connect with our deeper selves and empower us. Another way to do this is by using Reiki energy healing, particularly if the empath has experience with it already. It brings out the compassionate side that just wants to help others.

Attend a yoga or meditation class, where you can learn more about different techniques and find one that resonates with you. There is no need to be religious to do this - many people who are atheists or agnostics enjoy these practices.

Spending time in nature offers a sense of peace and connection. This could be taking a walk in the park, sitting by a lake, or simply looking at trees and flowers. It's all about finding what makes you feel good.

Creating a Daily Spiritual Routine

Once you have found out what works for you, it's important to create a daily spiritual routine. This could involve a combination of the things you have discovered, or it could be something completely different. The important thing is that it brings you joy and helps connect you with your spirit.

Some ideas to get started are:

- Prayer or meditation in the morning to set the tone for your day. This will help you stay centered and focused.

- A walk in nature or a quick stop at the park before going to work. It may seem insignificant, but it makes a difference!

- Sitting quietly for 20 minutes after dinner - or even right before bedtime. This is your time and no one else's, so block out any distractions from others as much as possible.

- Take a yoga or meditation class if you still feel like you're missing something. It could be that it's all about the community and support for others, which is just as important.

• Spending time with pets or plants (if they don't die on you). This brings out your nurturing side while also making you feel good about yourself.

Reaching Out to Others from a Place of Peace and Love

Lastly, it's important not only for the empath but for anyone, in general, to reach out and help others unconditionally – from a place of peace and love instead of fear or anxiety. This can be accomplished through volunteering at shelters, food banks, or even just by writing a letter to your local politician about an issue that matters to you.

The key is to do something that feels good in your heart and helps connect you with others in a positive way. Doing this opens up the door for more compassion and understanding in the world, which is what we need now more than ever.

When we connect to our spirit and embrace who we truly are, the world becomes a better place. We no longer feel like outsiders; instead, we become empowered to make a difference in the world.

The Benefits of Connecting with Your Spirit

• Feeling more at peace and content in life.

• Having a stronger sense of self-awareness and understanding yourself better.

• Being more compassionate and understanding towards others.

• Feeling a stronger connection to nature and the universe/all That's.

• Experiencing less anxiety and fear in life.

• Having a greater sense of inner wisdom and intuition.

- Finding joy in the little things, no matter what is going on around you.

- Being able to unconditionally love yourself – and others – from a place that does not judge or criticize but only wants to help. This means learning how to take care of ourselves first before we can help or support others.

- Being more empathetic and compassionate towards those who are suffering because we now know what it feels like for someone to judge us, criticize us, and find fault with everything that we do. We no longer feel the need to defend ourselves against these attacks; instead, we see them as opportunities to help others unconditionally.

We are all in this together, so let's have each other's backs and support one another through our Universal journey.

Meditation Methods

There are several types of meditation, and each has a different process. Some techniques may be more effective than others depending on the individual's personality, emotions, and lifestyle.

- **Sitting Method**

Sit in a comfortable position where you can see your belly rise and fall with each breath. Close your eyes. Start to follow the sensations of breathing, the coolness, pressure, or slight tickle as air passes through the nose on inhalation, and the feeling of greater ease when exhaling out past tension-filled areas like the throat and mouth.

Some people like to focus on a particular word, sound, or phrase to keep the mind present and not drift away with thoughts.

Other methods include repeating affirmations aloud while breathing in and releasing tension by saying "ahh" as you exhale. By chanting specific syllables such as "om," you can also connect with the energy of the universe.

- **Guided Visualization**

This is a process where you allow your imagination to take control and guide you on a journey. It can help explore different aspects of yourself or gain insight into a problem or situation.

You may want to find an audio recording, possibly from a yoga teacher or a meditation guide, where you can follow along with the words.

- **Sensory Method**

This is a guided practice using different senses to help relax and refocus on your body's present moment surroundings. You could also incorporate music when emotional memories arise by saying "ahh" as you exhale; this allows tension to release.

You could also incorporate different scents such as lavender or peppermint to help stimulate certain emotions associated with them, for example, using a calming scent when feeling stressed out.

- **Mindfulness Meditation**

This type of meditation focuses on breathing and being aware of each moment, here and now. It also clears your mind from ruminating thoughts that are not true or helpful.

You may want to start with focusing on one particular sensation during this process, such as how it feels when you inhale through your nostrils or notice the belly rising and falling.

Over time, you can add in different objects of focus such as sounds, physical sensations, or thoughts. You simply label the experience without judgment and let it pass on by.

- **Focused Meditation**

This type of meditation uses to focus. Focus on one particular thing or idea to cultivate more clarity and insight. For example, it could be a question that needs addressing, such as "what do I need to own about this situation?"

You can then visualize what the answer would look like once acknowledged, for instance, seeing a mental image of a new home.

- **Self-Inquiry**

This type of meditation is about finding the answer to who you are and what makes you unique within yourself. You can ask questions such as "what am I experiencing right now?" or "how do I want to feel?"

You can then turn these into positive affirmations such as "I am at peace" or "I trust my intuition."

The process of self-inquiry is also an opportunity to reflect on how you have been showing up in life and what changes could be made when the time is right.

- **Transcendental Meditation**

This is a more traditional style of meditation that involves repeating a mantra, such as an *om* or *peace*. It focuses on the breath and can be done by sitting upright in the lotus pose with hands on your knees. Alternatively, you could sit in a half-lotus position (one leg over the other).

To begin this technique, breathe in and out deeply a few times to relax before silently repeating your mantra. You should continue for around 20 minutes, but you can simply bring your focus back to the mantra if thoughts or distractions arise.

When you find a meditation technique that works for you, make sure to stick with it. Consistency is key to training the mind and developing a spiritual practice. You might also want to set some time aside each day to devote to your routine.

- **Practicing Forgiveness**

This is an important step on the spiritual path as it allows for a release of anger, resentment, and bitterness, all of which can build up and cause. It can be difficult to forgive someone who has hurt us deeply, but it's a powerful act that sets us free.

There are many different ways to approach forgiveness, such as writing a letter (but not sending it), imagining the person in your mind, or even just saying "I forgive you" aloud.

This practice allows for a renewed sense of peace and lets us put any past grievances behind us to move forward with more open hearts.

You may want to offer some guidance on how others might achieve forgiveness from those they have hurt.

Spiritual practices such as these can be incredibly transformative for empaths and highly sensitive people, imparting a sense of peace and connection often missing in our fast-paced world. When we take the time to slow down and connect with our innermost selves, we can access a deep well of wisdom and love that's always available to us.

- **Recognizing Your Creator**

This personal practice can be very powerful for empaths and HSPs. It involves looking at the world around you and seeing the divine fingerprints of God or the universe in everything.

This could be something as simple as noticing the beauty of a sunset or feeling moved by a song. It's about opening your heart and mind to the possibility that a higher power is at work in our lives, even when we can't see anything.

When we begin to recognize the divine in all things, it can bring about a sense of awe and wonder that touches our hearts deeply. It can also help us feel more connected to others and remind us that we are all part of something bigger than ourselves.

When we take the time to slow down and connect with our innermost selves, we can access a deep well of wisdom and love.

Being mindful of the Divine is a powerful way to recognize you are not alone and can give us a sense of meaning when we feel disconnected from others.

Whether or not you feel that you have been hurt by religion or God, you still can find solace in this form of meditation as well. People tend to forget that even non-believers can have a sense of spirituality.

- **Become More Accepting of Your Spirituality**

It's important to let go of any guilt or shame surrounding your spirituality, as this can prevent you from embracing it fully.

People raised in religious households may feel conflicted about their beliefs because they were taught that some things should be kept private. However, if you believe that there is something greater than yourself out there, it's worth exploring.

Accepting your spirituality means that you are open to the idea of greater power and are willing to learn more about it. This can be a journey that takes time and patience, but it's well worth the effort.

When we connect with our spirituality, we tap into a deep source of compassion and love that's always available to us. Embrace this connection and allow it to guide you on your path in life.

- **Practicing Spiritual Reflection**

One of the best ways to connect with your spirituality is by practicing spiritual reflection. This involves taking some time each day to sit in silence and simply be with your thoughts.

You may want to focus on your breath or allow yourself to wander freely through your mind. The important thing is not judging or criticizing yourself but simply observing what comes up.

Practicing this form of reflection helps you to find peace and clarity amid chaos, providing a calm center to return to when your mind is overwhelmed by outside stimuli.

This could be difficult for empaths who are constantly bombarded by outside stimuli. It might be best to suggest that they try this practice in a quiet room or out in nature where there aren't as many distractions as possible.

Spiritual reflection can help us connect with our inner selves and heal any feelings of disconnection we have from other people, the universe,

It's also a great way for empaths and HSPs to cope with busy social lives or volatile emotions that might otherwise feel overwhelming.

When we take the time to slow down and connect with our innermost selves, we can access a deep well of wisdom and love that's always available to us.

- **Accepting Your Faults**

It's also important to accept your faults and work on making positive changes.

Nobody is perfect, and we all have things we need to work on. This includes empaths and HSPs.

It can be a powerful step towards change when you acknowledge your faults. It can also help you feel more connected to others and remind you that we all struggle with different things.

Being honest about our shortcomings will help us learn from past mistakes and avoid repeating them in the future. It also means being willing to ask for help when you need it.

This could be difficult, as many empaths pride themselves on their independence and do not want to appear weak. However, it's important to remember that we are all human, and no one can do everything on their own.

We become humbler and more compassionate towards ourselves and others when we accept our faults. This creates a foundation of self-love that can be built upon over time.

Embracing your spirituality is an important step on the path to self-discovery.

- **Recognizing the Goodness in Others**

Another important part of embracing your spirituality is recognizing the goodness in others.

When we seek out the best in people, we will connect with them on a deeper level. It also helps us build positive relationships and create a more peaceful world.

This can be difficult for the empath, who are often more sensitive to negative environments and difficult personalities.

However, don't assume the worst of somebody before you know their intentions. Everyone has a different way of thinking or acting that might seem strange from an outsider's perspective, but it only reflects who they really are on the inside.

You can help by avoiding gossip, judgmental thoughts, and negative comments. Try to see the good in others before you pass judgment on anything they do or say.

Being more open-minded can help you empathize with people who might seem different from you at first glance. It also helps foster a sense of unity that's critical for creating positive change in our world.

- **The Power of Writing a Journal**

One way to embrace your spirituality is by writing in a journal.

When we take the time to express our thoughts and feelings, it can be incredibly liberating. It also allows us to reflect on our lives and see how we've changed over time.

Journaling can also help us connect with our intuition and access information that might not otherwise be available to us.

This is a great spiritual tool that can help empaths in many different ways! It's also a wonderful way for children, teens, or highly sensitive people with disabilities to express themselves when they might not have the words to do so verbally.

In addition, journaling can help us see the good in others and notice how we've grown.

It can be difficult to find time to write every day, especially when you have other responsibilities like school or work that take up your energy. However, everyone needs to make time for self-reflection at least once a week – if not more often.

Journaling can also be a great way to find your spiritual center and connect with the world around you on a deeper level. Try it out for yourself, even if you feel like you're not ready yet! It's never too late to explore who you are as an individual.

- **Hobbies and Activities that Connect You with Your Spiritual Side**

Many different activities and hobbies can help you connect to your spiritual side.

Some people enjoy going for walks in nature, while others might prefer to meditate or read religious texts. There is no wrong way to do this!

The important thing is that the activity brings you joy and allows you to connect with your inner self.

This could be something as simple as coloring, crafting, or taking photos. It's up to you to find what works best for you!

Empaths often have a naturally strong connection to their spiritual side, which can manifest in different ways but is most commonly characterized by a deep sense of compassion and humility.

When we embrace our spirituality, we become more connected to the world around us. We also learn to love ourselves for who we are, warts and all. This creates a foundation of self-love that can be built upon over time.

Conclusion

People often struggle with ideas such as self-identity, self-awareness, self-image, and nearly everything that has to do with self-analysis is a challenge. This is largely because they either don't have the tools to self-evaluate, or they don't have the patience to go through the process and simply accept reality as is without any judgment. The reality is that we don't choose how we want to be. We are all born with gifts, tendencies, behaviors, and even a mindset. The great thing is that this doesn't have to be the rest of your life. You can make the changes you want to see, and even if you can't completely change the way you are as a person, you can still develop a lot of control over how you are and how you manage your strengths and weaknesses. Throughout this book, we have looked at some of the best ways for you to highlight your strengths and weaknesses, which will help you get a better understanding of what kind of an empath or a highly sensitive person you are.

The other main challenge most people have in life is dealing with different circumstances. Specifically, they don't know how they can steer themselves in such a way that they benefit from what is going on, and they leverage their innate abilities and strengths. Being a highly sensitive person or an empath is not bad, but the difference is in how you use this skill. If you approach it the right way, it can work in your favor and give you the competitive advantage you need. If you fail to recognize your abilities and you work in a way that you are going against the grain, it will only make it harder for you and possibly also make it harder for the people around you.

Using the tips and techniques that we have covered in this book, you can ensure that you excel in every aspect of life. More importantly, as a teacher, parent, worker, or friend, you can develop deeper and more meaningful relationships while also looking out for yourself. Empaths have an incredible set of talents and unique abilities that can make them excel in every area of life, however at the same time, they are also prone to a few problems, and they have some challenges that others won't understand. If you are careful about managing the highly sensitive person inside you, life can be made so much easier. This doesn't have to be a drastic change; slowly and gradually, you can work on yourself, start to build on your strengths, and try to guard against your weaknesses.

Living a happy and fulfilling life is more than just fulfilling your desires. Even if you can get everything that you always wanted, but you are still not comfortable in your own skin, those material objects will not give you the satisfaction or happiness you hoped for. To achieve real peace, you need to achieve peace within yourself and understand who you are rather than just following the herd. You are in control of your life, and it's the only one you get, so make the decision today to improve your conditions.

Here's another book by Silvia Hill that you might like

Free limited time bonus

Stop for a moment. I have a free bonus set up for you. The problem is that we forget 90% of everything that we read after 7 days. Crazy fact, right? Here's the solution: we've created a printable, 1-page pdf summary for this book that you're reading now. All you have to do to get your free pdf summary is to go to the following website: **https://livetolearn.lpages.co/silviahill/**
Once you do, it will be intuitive. Enjoy, and thank you!

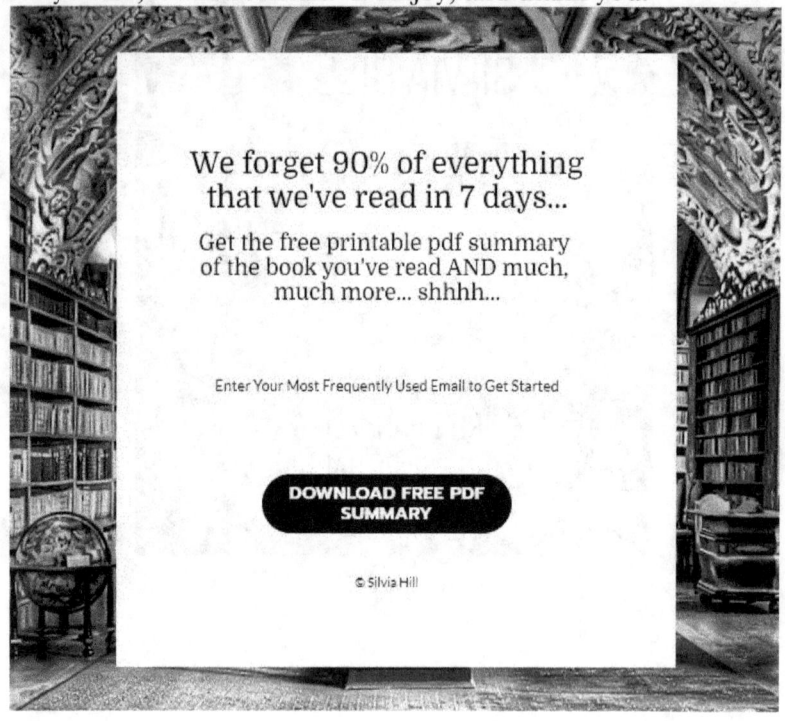

References

Baker, J. (2021, August 10). The three kinds of empathy: Emotional, cognitive, and

compassionate. Sacred Structures by Jim Baker. https://sacredstructures.org/messages/the-three-kinds-of-empathy-emotional-cognitive-and-compassionate

Bariso, J. (2018, September 19). There are actually 3 types of empathy. Here's how they differ--and how you can develop them all. Inc. https://www.inc.com/justin-bariso/there-are-actually-3-types-of-empathy-heres-how-they-differ-and-how-you-can-develop-them-all.html

Campbell, L. (n.d.). What is an empath, and how do you know if you are one? Verywell Mind. Retrieved from https://www.verywellmind.com/what-is-an-empath-and-how-do-you-know-if-you-are-one-5119883

Firestone, L. (2017, March 28). Empaths: Is being an empath a superpower or a super-stressor?

PsychAlive.

https://www.psychalive.org/empaths

Parpworth-Reynolds, C. (2020, May 13). 10 famous empaths – some of these may surprise you. Subconscious Servant. https://subconsciousservant.com/famous-empaths

Raypole, C. (2019, November 25). What is an empath? 15 signs and traits. Healthline. https://www.healthline.com/health/what-is-an-empath

Regan, S. (2021, August 16). Think you could be an empath? 12 signs to watch out for & what it really means. Mindbodygreen. https://www.mindbodygreen.com/articles/empath

Sólo, A. (2019, January 18). 13 signs that you're an empath. Highly Sensitive Refuge. https://highlysensitiverefuge.com/empath-signs/

What is empathy? Learn about 3 types of empathy. (2020, June 24). TakeAltus. https://takealtus.com/2020/06/empathy-1

Are you an introverted or extroverted empath? (2018, June 29). Retrieved from Judith Orloff MD website: https://drjudithorloff.com/ask-dr-orloff/are-all-empaths-introverts

Athar, K. (2020, November 29). 16 signs you're an introverted empath (and 5 tips to make life easier). Retrieved from Nomadrs website: https://nomadrs.com/introverted-empath

LindstromExpert, B., & 02/06/, S. (2021, February 6). 11 Types Of Empaths – and how to know which one you Are. Retrieved from YourTango website: https://www.yourtango.com/experts/brittney-lindstrom/read-if-you-want-know-what-type-empath-you-are

Stamatinos, A. (2016, September 23). 10 Reasons Being An Empath Is A gift. Retrieved from The Minds Journal website: https://themindsjournal.com/being-an-empath-gift

Valko, L. (2019, November 29). 14 problems only empaths will understand. Retrieved from Highly Sensitive Refuge website: https://highlysensitiverefuge.com/14-problems-only-empaths-will-understand

Deadwiler, A. (2018, October 18). Life of an empath. Retrieved from Medium website:

https://acamea.medium.com/life-of-an-empath-cda7da43da10

Valko, L. (2019, November 29). 14 problems only empaths will understand. Retrieved from Highly Sensitive Refuge website: https://highlysensitiverefuge.com/14-problems-only-empaths-will-understand

Are you an HSP or Empath. What's the difference? (n.d.). Empathdiary.Com. Retrieved from

https://www.empathdiary.com/messages/are-you-an-empath

Are you highly sensitive? (n.d.). Hsperson.Com. Retrieved from

https://hsperson.com/test/highly-sensitive-test

Bell, E. (2018, April 26). What it means to be a Highly Sensitive Person or HSP. The Anxious Empath. https://emmaclairebell.com/highly-sensitive-person-hsp

Dodgson, L. (2019, January 7). The difference between empaths, highly sensitive people, and introverts. Insider. https://www.insider.com/difference-between-empaths-highly-sensitive-people-and-introverts-2018-6

Funniest Empath Quiz & More. (n.d.). Empathdiary.Com. Retrieved from

https://www.empathdiary.com/quiz

Granneman, J. (2015, July 8). Are you highly sensitive? {Take the Highly Sensitive Person Test}. IntrovertDear.Com. https://introvertdear.com/news/highly-sensitive-person-test-quiz

Granneman, J. (2019, December 13). 21 signs that you're a highly sensitive person (HSP). Highly Sensitive Refuge. https://highlysensitiverefuge.com/highly-sensitive-person-signs

Harrison, T. (2020, December 24). Are you A true empath or just sensitive? Take this quiz to find out. The Minds Journal. https://themindsjournal.com/empath-or-hsp-quiz

Hollywood, J. (2014, August 24). Empath: 8 signs you might be one (with quiz). Exemplore.

https://exemplore.com/paranormal/Empath-Self-Assessment-8-Common-Traits-of-Empathic-People-with-Pictures

MelwaniExpert, K., & 08/27/, S. (2020, August 27). How to tell if you're A Highly Sensitive

Person (HSP) or an empath. YourTango.

https://www.yourtango.com/experts/kavita-melwani/are-you-highly-sensitive-person-hsp-empath-how-tell-difference

Sólo, A. (2020, June 17). The difference between introverts, empaths, and highly sensitive people. Highly Sensitive Refuge. https://highlysensitiverefuge.com/empaths-highly-sensitive-people-introverts

Ursano, I. (2019, February 4). Are you A highly sensitive person or an empath? Find out now. Amazing Me Movement. https://amazingmemovement.com/highly-sensitive-person-quiz

What type of details usually caught your attention? (2021, September 11). Quiz Expo.

https://www.quizexpo.com/wpqquestionpnt/what-type-of-details-usually-caught-your-attention

Wright, S. (2020, November 20). Am I highly sensitive, an empath, or just shy? – Perspectives Holistic Therapy.

https://www.perspectivesholistictherapy.com/blog-posts/2020/11/20/am-i-a-highly-sensitive-person-empath

Empaths and addiction: From alcohol to overeating. (n.d.). Psychology Today. Retrieved from https://www.psychologytoday.com/us/blog/the-empaths-survival-guide/201906/empaths-and-addiction-alcohol-overeating

How does being an empath have to do with addiction? (n.d.). Lastresortrecovery.Com. Retrieved from https://www.lastresortrecovery.com/addiction-blog/what-does-being-an-empath-have-to-do-with-addiction

deBara, D. (2021, July 9). 8 jobs that are great for empaths (and 3 that typically Aren't). The Muse. https://www.themuse.com/advice/jobs-careers-for-empaths

Empathintheoffice.Com. Retrieved from https://www.empathintheoffice.com/blog/how-to-work-for-a-controlling-boss

Brady, K. (2019, July 24). Being an empath: 7 ways to stop absorbing other people's emotions. Keir Brady Counseling Services. https://www.keirbradycounseling.com/empath-and-absorbing-other-peoples-emotions

Nasamran, A. (2021, March 1). Highly sensitive child parenting strategies. Atlas Psychology. https://www.atlaspsychologycollective.com/blog/highly-sensitive-child-parenting-strategies

Clarke, J., MA, & LPC/MHSP. (n.d.). Covert narcissist: Signs, causes, and how to respond. Verywell Mind. Retrieved from https://www.verywellmind.com/understanding-the-covert-narcissist-4584587

Dodgson, L. (2018, January 23). Empaths and narcissists make a "toxic" partnership – here's why they're attracted to each other. Insider. https://www.businessinsider.com/why-empaths-and-narcissists-are-attracted-to-each-other-2018-1

Stone, J. (2018). Narcissistic personality disorder: An unbiased psychological study of Donald trump. Createspace Independent Publishing Platform.

Bock, H. (2018, January 30). 5 telltale signs an empath is overwhelmed. Linkedin.Com;

LinkedIn. https://www.linkedin.com/pulse/5-telltale-signs-empath-overwhelmed-halley-bock

Michaela. (2020, August 19). 6 ways to cope with empath overwhelm. Introvert Spring.

https://introvertspring.com/6-ways-to-cope-with-empath-overwhelm

Anastasia. (2018, July 1). 7 boundary exercises for empaths and sensitive people. Kind Earth. https://www.kindearth.net/7-boundary-exercises-for-empaths-and-other-sensitive-people

Margarita Tartakovsky, M. S. (2018, December 9). How empathic people can set effective, loving boundaries. Psych Central. https://psychcentral.com/blog/how-empathic-people-can-set-effective-loving-boundaries

Brady, K. (2019, July 24). Being an empath: 7 ways to stop absorbing other people's emotions. Keir Brady Counseling Services. https://www.keirbradycounseling.com/empath-and-absorbing-other-peoples-emotions

Raypole, C. (2020, April 28). How to control your emotions: 11 strategies to try. Healthline. https://www.healthline.com/health/how-to-control-your-emotions

Anastasia. (2018, July 1). 7 boundary exercises for empaths and sensitive people. Kind Earth.

https://www.kindearth.net/7-boundary-exercises-for-empaths-and-other-sensitive-people

Are you a physical empath? (n.d.). Psychology Today. Retrieved from

https://www.psychologytoday.com/us/blog/the-ecstasy-surrender/201402/are-you-physical-empath?amp

Cooks-Campbell, A. (2021, December 8). Why are empathy fatigue and compassion fatigue so common? Betterup.Com.

https://www.betterup.com/blog/empathy-and-compassion-fatigue?hs_amp=true

Duan, H., Wang, Y.-J., & Lei, X. (2021). The effect of sleep deprivation on empathy for pain: An ERP study. Neuropsychologia, 163(108084), 108084.

https://doi.org/10.1016/j.neuropsychologia.2021.108084

hollow. (2021, June 25). Empathy fatigue: How stress and trauma can take a toll on you. Cleveland Clinic. https://health.clevelandclinic.org/empathy-fatigue-how-stress-and-trauma-can-take-a-toll-on-you

The energy of empathy. (2019, November 30). The Eden Magazine.

https://theedenmagazine.com/the-energy-of-empathy

Valko, L. (2019, November 29). 14 problems only empaths will understand. Highly Sensitive Refuge. https://highlysensitiverefuge.com/14-problems-only-empaths-will-understand

Alison, A. L. (2020). Empath Workbook: Discover 50 successful tips to boost your emotional,

physical, and spiritual energy. Alison L. Alverson.

Annesley, C. (2020). Empath: Beginner's guide to improve your empathy skills, increase self-esteem, protect yourself from energy vampires, and overcome fears (a guide to protecting yourself against energy vampires and narcissists). Harry Stewart.

Fairygodboss. (2019, September 20). 5 ways for empaths to manage tough work situations. Insider. https://www.businessinsider.com/5-ways-for-empaths-to-manage-tough-work-situations-2019-9

Hope, A. (2021). Empath healing: A short guide to finding your sense of self and understanding highly sensitive people's emotional abilities to feel empathy and deal with energy vampires. Creative Publishing Solution.

Levenson, R. W., & Ruef, A. M. (1992). Empathy: a physiological substrate. Journal of

Personality and Social Psychology, 63(2), 234–246.

https://doi.org/10.1037//0022-3514.63.2.234